Company Towle Mfg.

Georgian

A Pattern of Spoons, Forks and all other Pieces of Table Flat Ware is Partly

Shown in This Book

Company Towle Mfg.

Georgian

A Pattern of Spoons, Forks and all other Pieces of Table Flat Ware is Partly Shown in This Book

ISBN/EAN: 9783337125561

Printed in Europe, USA, Canada, Australia, Japan

Cover: Foto ©Andreas Hilbeck / pixelio.de

More available books at **www.hansebooks.com**

Georgian

A pattern of spoons, forks
and all other pieces of ✣ Table Flat
Ware ✣ is partly shown in this book, in
which is also given an account of the chief
events of the War of the Revolution
and the acts of oppression which preceded
and provoked it; ✣ to which are added sundry
pictures of Places and Things identified
with this momentous conflict ✣ and in some
cases exemplifying the Colonial, or most
properly called Georgian style of architecture, from which the design of this pattern
is derived; which style was first produced in
England in the eighteenth century and
was the result of an adaptation of classical
elements to new conditions of application, and
all of which is ap- purtenant to the
name and times of

By the KING,

A PROCLAMATION,

For fuppreffing Rebellion and Sedition.

GEORGE R.

WHEREAS many of Our Subjects in divers Parts of Our Colonies and Plantations in *North America*, mifled by dangerous and ill-defigning Men, and forgetting the Allegiance which they owe to the Power that has protected and fuftained them, after various diforderly Acts committed in Difturbance of the Publick Peace, to the Obftruction of lawful Commerce, and to the Oppreffion of Our loyal Subjects carrying on the fame, have at length proceeded to an open and avowed Rebellion, by arraying themfelves in hoftile Manner to withftand the Execution of the Law, and traitoroufly preparing, ordering, and levying War againft Us; And whereas there is Reafon to apprehend that fuch Rebellion hath been much promoted and encouraged by the traiterous Correfpondence, Counfels, and Comfort of divers wicked and defperate Perfons within this Realm : To the End therefore that none of Our Subjects may neglect or violate their Duty through Ignorance thereof, or through any Doubt of the Protection which the Law will afford to their Loyalty and Zeal; We have thought fit, by and with the Advice of Our Privy Council, to iffue this Our Royal Proclamation, hereby declaring that not only all Our Officers Civil and Military are obliged to exert their utmoft Endeavours to fupprefs fuch Rebellion, and to bring the Traitors to Juftice ; but that all Our Subjects of this Realm and the Dominions thereunto belonging are bound by Law to be aiding and affifting in the Suppreffion of fuch Rebellion, and to difclofe and make known all traitorous Confpiracies and Attempts againft Us, Our Crown and Dignity ; And We do accordingly ftrictly charge and command all Our Officers as well Civil as Military, and all other Our obedient and loyal Subjects, to ufe their utmoft Endeavours to withftand and fuppref fuch Rebellion, and to difclofe and make known all Treafons and traitorous Confpiracies which they fhall know to be againft Us, Our Crown and Dignity ; and for that Purpofe, that they tranfmit to One of Our Principal Secretaries of State, or other proper Officer, due and full Information of all Perfons who fhall be found carrying on Correfpondence with, or in any Manner or Degree aiding or abetting the Perfons now in open Arms, and Rebellion againft Our Government within any of Our Colonies and Plantations in *North America* in order to bring to condign Punifhment the Authors, Perpetrators, and Abettors of fuch traitorous Defigns.

Given at Our Court at St *James*'s, the Twenty-third Day of *Auguft*, One thoufand feven hundred and feventy-five, in the Fifteenth Year of Our Reign.

God fave the King.

L O N D O N
Printed by *Charles Eyre* and *William Strahan*, Printers to the King's moft Excellent Majefty. 1775.

O N the outskirts of Portsmouth, New Hampshire, by the water's edge, stands a picturesque old mansion that will, if we are so minded, carry us backward, at one step, to the "Old Colony days" when George III ruled over the English people on both sides of the Atlantic.

It was built by Governor Benning Wentworth, and from under its roof issued those first edicts of oppression that stirred the people to revolt. Within its walls one needs but little help from fancy to people it again with loyal retainers, assembled, perhaps, in its ancient council chamber, with ample chimney-piece, the carven heads of which might, could they exercise the privilege of their sex, reveal many a bit of inner history. We are prosaic indeed if we do not feel the menace of sudden alarms suggested by the grim array of muskets on either side of the stoutly barred door ; and the discovery of a prisoner's ward, tucked away in a remote corner, should complete a realization of the stern conditions of life in the eighteenth century.

It is not our purpose, however, to linger in this house, fascinating though it be, but to pass through it from the world of to-day to the times it so vividly recalls. Two names that are intimately connected with it will readily take us across the ocean, and back through a century and more, to the court of the king whose misguided policy was the birth-warrant of our nation. One of these we find in Newcastle, separated by a devious inlet from Little Harbor — where Governor Wentworth built — and reminiscent of the Duke of Newcastle who was prime minister of England and leader of the Whig party at the beginning of the Revolutionary period. A few years later, after the turn of events had deprived him of power, he again entered the cabinet with the post of privy seal under the leadership of the Marquis of Rockingham, a member of the Wentworth family, for whom Governor Wentworth had named the county back of Portsmouth and Newcastle.

Although nominally representative of the people, Parliament was in those days the creature of its leaders, or the King, as successive complications favored one or the other ; boroughs were bought or bullied by the dominant party, and thus the momentous enactments that goaded the colonists to revolt were the results of contested intrigue, a game with living pieces and tremendous stakes, played by the government and the opposition, and in which the English people had little real voice.

The conception of the odious Stamp Act is credited to Jenkinson, secretary to Lord Bute, the King's favored minister ; but Parlia-ment rejected it when first

Stamp

An Old House

Governor Wentworth House

Portsmouth N. H.

proposed, although it was universally conceded that America should contribute to the payment of the enormous public debt contracted in the protection of the colonies from the French and Indians. Even Americans acquiesced in this sentiment, but they proposed to pay it by grants from their assemblies and in their own way. George, however, had been exhorted by his mother, the Princess Dowager, to "be a king" and encouraged to assert his individuality — advice which conditions did not favor, nor the King's ability warrant, but which he persistently endeavored to carry out in spite of its disastrous effect. Under these circumstances the proposition to *1765* levy a stamp tax was revived and the act passed in February, 1765. William Pitt, the constant champion of the colonies, was ill at the time, and greatly deplored its passage. Throughout the remainder of his life, which ended while the war was in *1778* progress, Pitt, afterwards Lord Chatham, was an ardent advocate of the liberties of the colonists; but his efforts were of little avail, and although he was at one time urged by the King to form a ministry, many concessions being made to induce him to do so, personal ambition and the resulting internal friction had so divided his party that he was unable to unite the leaders, and the policy then in force was suffered to continue.

In America the Stamp Act was resented as a measure of arbitrary domination, an irritating and unreasonable form of taxation with no compensatory representation. Virginia was the first colony to voice the opposition to this measure, and was immediately followed by Massachusetts, which proposed a congress of delegates from the *1765* assemblies of all the colonies to take united action in protest. The congress met in 1765, and as a result of this, and Pitt's scathing denunciation in England, the Stamp *1766* Act was repealed early in the following year.

The King from this time lost no opportunity of strengthening his party in Parliament, and by the patronage he could dispense and the intimidation of country boroughs, was able to control both houses and secure the enactment of his policy. His next measure was the levying of import duties on colonial commerce, which was

The Stamp Act

growing rapidly in importance, especially with the West Indies; and with England alone amounted to about six million pounds per year, nearly equalling the total of British commerce with the world at the beginning of that century. This also met with bitter protest and was later repealed on everything but tea, which was made to bear the burden of the principle of English sovereignty. This principle was as clearly discerned in America as in England, and the renunciation of tea became a test of patriotism. Philadelphia had publicly denounced all traffic in tea, and the act had been endorsed by Boston when three ships laden with the obnoxious commodity arrived at the latter port. Their arrival was followed by indignant gatherings in Faneuil Hall, and the consignees were forced by public opinion to promise that the ships would be sent back without unloading; but this the Royal Governor refused to permit, and declared that no clearance papers would be issued until the cargoes were discharged. At the close of a particularly demonstrative meeting held at the Old South Church on the afternoon of December sixteenth, 1773, a party of fifty citizens, disguised as Indians, led the way to the wharf, and, boarding the vessels, scattered into the harbor the contents of three hundred and forty-two chests, the property of the East India Company, valued in the neighborhood of one hundred thousand dollars.

In consequence of this action and lesser excuses, Massachusetts was subjected to a repressive policy which deprived the colonists of many liberties and was intended to precipitate a struggle, which the King believed would be short and decisive, for the purpose of finally settling the dependence of the colonies and the sovereignty of England.

The effect of this "Port Bill," as the chief of these measures was called, was — as was expected — to confirm the colonists in their resistance, but not in the rash and isolated way that was hoped for. Keen, powerful intellects guided the people, in the persons of Samuel Adams, John Adams, Robert Treat Paine, and others, and they immediately set about to secure the coöperation of the other colonies, many of which were ripe for action, notably Virginia, where Patrick

Chimney-piece
Council Chamber

Wentworth House

Stamp

Boston Tea Party

Henry had some years earlier openly denounced British oppression, but had lacked the clear issues prevalent in the Bay State. They organized a Committee of Correspondence, and, authorized by the General Assembly of Massachusetts, urged each colony to send delegates to a congress at Philadelphia on the first of the following September.

In June of that year, 1774, the port of Boston, then under the military rule of General Gage — who had superseded Governor Hutchinson — was closed to commerce, causing a complete stagnation of business of all kinds, and much deprivation and suffering among the people.

A considerable element in Parliament was strongly opposed to this cruelty, and champions of the cause of America were not lacking who predicted the ultimate ruin England would suffer from this unwarranted oppression of her own sons, to whom, as they urged, the sentiments of liberty were as precious, and whose strength of purpose was as great, as though no ocean separated them from the free institutions of the mother country. They were powerless, however, to check the wave of vindictiveness that now, under the fostering care of the King's favorites, was extending even to the people.

The large cities, always the strongholds of advanced ideas, were still in sympathy with the colonists, and the spectacle is presented of the city of London, in its corporate capacity, subscribing one hundred and fifty thousand dollars for the relief of suffering in Boston, caused by the acts of Parliament. These were eventful days in the New England town, for although the people suffered, their enthusiasm was in no way diminished, and they overthrew all civil institutions emanating from the crown.

Hancock House
Boston Mass

Many prominent people who had until this time reserved the right to support the King's government and hoped for a peaceful settlement of all troubles, now saw the seriousness of the situation, and realizing the near approach of inevitable division, sank their personal regrets in love of country and joined heartily in the cause of liberty.

On the fifth of September, fifty-three delegates assembled in Carpenter's Hall, Philadelphia, and under the presidency of Peyton Randolph, of Virginia, formed a Continental Congress. While recognizing the necessity of united action, these delegates, as a whole, had not yet reached a realization of the need of aggressive rebellion. The habit of loyalty was too strong to be put off at once, and it was with a certain deference, albeit firmness, that they appealed to the King, and to the people of Great Britain, to withdraw the odious measures that threatened to alienate the colonies. Georgia, the especial protégé of the King, was alone unrepresented at this gathering, and though at

First Continental Congress

heart the delegates dreaded the culmination of events which their acts were forwarding, the congress adopted measures to strengthen the union and co-operation of the states, indorsed Massachusetts in its resistance, and planned and appointed a second congress to meet the following May. Although independence was not yet declared, and, in the minds of many, was only a remote possibility, it was in reality inaugurated on that twentieth of October, 1774, when the "Declaration of Colonial Rights," a comprehensive document which recited the injustices of Parliament and asserted the right of self-government, was signed by the "American Association," the forerunner of the confederacy later announced as the "United States of America."

Faneuil Hall

Boston Mass.

1774

As seed cast on fertile ground germinates and develops of its innate powers, so the American Revolution needed but the lightest sanction of administrative authority. Its real life was the unwavering determination of individuals and communities to meet squarely every issue, to see great principles behind even small aggressions, to neither palliate nor compromise, to rise above considerations of policy and to act from the first with no provision for failure and no desire for qualified victory.

Separation from the mother country was but incidental to this struggle, and was only determined upon when in the progress of events it was recognized as inevitable. The principles of liberty for which the patriots contended were no less applicable here than in England itself, where their kinsmen had declared and enacted them nearly a century before.

This spirit was manifest, but it was King George, with his succession of blundering provocations, who nourished the Revolution. Had he realized the quality of the resistance and listened to the entreatings of Franklin and the other colonial agents at Parliament, he could easily have retained that loyalism which was dear to the colonists, and the price of which was only the extension of equal liberty to his subjects at home and abroad.

Although at this time the Americans were endeavoring to obtain a peaceful establishment of their rights, they clearly perceived the need of military organization, and in November the "Provincial Congress" of Massachusetts, — the General Court under a new name — voted to enroll twelve thousand "minute men" who were to be prepared to respond immediately when the conflict should begin ; later it declared its wish for peace, but advised preparations for war. Other colonies took similar

The "American Association"

Old Powder Tower Somerville Mass.

action and many minor episodes took place which are locally held to be the initiative of the Revolution. December sixth, the people of Rhode Island seized a large quantity of ordnance in the batteries at Newport, in anticipation of its employment by the King's troops, and the same action was taken on the thirteenth by the people of Portsmouth, New Hampshire, who seized and removed a large quantity of ammunition and ordnance then in the keeping of the garrison of Fort William and Mary, at Newcastle. In the following February, the people of Salem, Massachusetts, taking heed from the warning of their governing body, began preparations for defense. These were met by an expedition from Gage's forces at Boston, and an engagement was narrowly averted. The real uprising, however, from which armed rebellion dates, was to come later at Concord and Lexington.

Parliament had officially declared a state of rebellion existent in Massachusetts and embarked large reinforcements to the three thousand British troops in Boston, while the patriots watched every movement of the British and prepared to meet their first advance, which in the nature of things could not long be delayed. General Gage, the British commander, realized it to be his duty to break up these preparations, and planned a secret raid on the stores and munitions which the Americans had concentrated at Concord, some miles from Boston, in order that they might be safely outside the line of fortifications which the British were erecting. The plan also included the capture of John Hancock and Samuel Adams, who were believed to be in that neighborhood, and who were justly regarded as most dangerous to British interests. With this object troops to the number of eight hundred left Boston for Cambridge shortly before midnight of April eighteenth, and with such speed as was possible, marched toward Lexington, on the road to Concord. They had counted on the secrecy of their movements to make the attainment of their object easy, but in this they underestimated the watchfulness and penetration of their opponents, for their purpose was understood in advance and measures taken to spread the alarm when they should actually start.

Paul Revere had obtained the information, and he repaired to Charlestown that evening, there to await the signal which he had directed to be shown from the spire of the North Church when the soldiers were known to have started. The two lights, telling him that they had gone by water to Cambridge, shone out at eleven o'clock and started Revere on his momentous ride. He was obliged to take a circuitous route to escape British sentinels, who challenged him and who would have captured a less alert man. In spite of this he gained a great advance over the attacking force, and alarmed the country to Lexington, where he awakened Adams and Hancock, and was joined by two others in his ride toward Concord. They were hardly started when they were intercepted by British officers and Revere and Dawes were taken prisoners,

New England Flag

Early Acts

while Dr. Prescott, the third member of the party, jumped his horse over a wall and escaped to carry the alarm the remainder of the way.

What it meant to the farmers was evident when, early in the morning, the regulars reached Lexington and found the minute-men drawn up on the green to meet them. Compared with the British, the patriots were few and were poorly equipped and drilled, but their cause was righteous and they believed in it in the face of death. They, therefore, paid no heed to the demand that they dis-

Kings Chapel Boston Mass *1775*

perse, but met force with force and shed the first blood of the Revolution. Eight Americans were killed and others wounded, and the British then continued their march to Concord. Their commander, Lieutenant-Colonel Smith, alarmed by the evidences of resistance that he encountered, had sent back to Boston for reinforcements, which were hastening to his assistance.

Their mission at Concord was accomplished ingloriously to the extent of destroying such few stores and guns as the Americans had been unable to secrete, and they were about to return when they discovered the minute-men advancing from the farther side of the North Bridge. They essayed to cut off the approach of the Americans by removing the bridge, but were too late, and, being obliged to retreat or fire, chose the latter, and were answered by a volley which drove them from their position. This was the beginning of the first real fight, the passage at Lexington being hardly maintained to an extent to justify that title. The farmers withdrew to such shelter as they could find and awaited further movements of the regulars, who started about noon for their return to Boston. Their march was the signal for renewed firing by the Americans, who followed them, and from the shelter of stone walls and trees delivered a harassing and destructive fire.

Thoroughly routed, they were fast being reduced when they were met by the advancing reinforcements, one thousand men under Lord Percy, and for a while they rested under this protection. The remainder of the retreat, even with the greatly increased force, was a repetition of the beginning, and when they finally arrived in Charlestown, and under the guns of the British ships, they were in almost a panic.

Thus began the Revolution; and the alarm carried by Paul Revere was extended in all directions until every road leading to Concord was filled with minute-men hastening to reinforce their compatriots. They remained in waiting a few days,

Concord and Lexington

but no further attack being made they returned to their homes for completer organ-ization and equipment. They realized that the struggle which was now begun meant systematic operations of defense, for which they were as yet unprepared, and an army was recruited and established in Cambridge to be ready for such action as might be necessary.

In the meantime the Massachusetts delegation to the second Congress had journeyed, in a succession of ovations, to Philadelphia, and were assured of the approval and support of the intervening colonies. May tenth, the day this Congress opened, *1775* was signalized, though the members knew not of it, by the capture of Ticonderoga by an expedition from Connecticut under Colonel Ethan Allen, and a large quantity of ammunition and ordnance was turned over to the army. Events were moving rapidly without Congress, but it was essential that there be a central authority to out-line the policy to be pursued and provide means for effecting it. Even now Con-gress distrusted its own right to be, and repeated its supplications to George III to settle without further bloodshed the differences that existed.

These entreatings evidence the reluctance of the delegates to forswear their allegiance to England, but the fact that they nevertheless took such measures as were possible to organize and equip an army is proof also of their steadiness of purpose and desperate belief in the worthiness of their cause.

Old South Church Boston Mass.

The first important act of Congress was the appoint-ment of George Washington, one of the delegates from Virginia, commander-in-chief of the American army, which was then, to the number of upwards of fifteen thou-sand men, encamped in the vicinity of Boston.

This army, recruited by the Provincial Congress of Massachusetts, was made up of the minute-men who had risen on the alarm of Lexington, but who had, in the meantime, returned to their homes for reorganization, and later volunteers, with considerable reinforcements from neighboring states, notably New Hampshire and Con-necticut; and under the leadership of officers whose names are now the foundations of Revolutionary history, was besieging Boston and planning to drive out the British, or at least to prevent them from increasing their holdings.

While Washington was preparing to start for New England, events in Boston were rapidly shaping them-selves for the active operations of war. General Gage, the British commander, was forced to take measures to maintain his position, and determined to forestall the Americans in the occupation of Charlestown, across the river, and so near his headquarters that he was liable at any time to be subjected to a harassing fire. His plans were disturbed, however, by the dis-covery, on the morning of June seventeenth, of fortifications which the Americans had thrown up on Bunker Hill in one short night. It had become known to the American commanders that Gage contemplated moving on the eighteenth, and over a thousand hardy and intelligent men, under skillful direction, worked with pick and shovel from the settling of darkness on the sixteenth to the dawn of the seventeenth, and then, with slight reinforcements, awaited the attack of the British.

Medford   Mass.

Prescott, Warren, Stark, and Knowlton were among the American commanders, and by their personal bravery and perseverance they sustained the courage of their men, with the result that the British attacking force of three thousand, with all its perfect equipment, was twice repulsed with fearful loss, and only yielded to after a third destructive charge, and when the last round of their meagre ammunition was exhausted.   Under the cover of a protecting fire from a line of auxiliary defense, a part of the original plan, the Americans retreated and left the British in possession of one of the most dearly bought battle-fields of history.   The British loss was enormous, and this engagement prevented further aggression beyond the limits of their original holding.   It also resulted in the superseding of Gage by General Howe, as commander of all the British forces.   The news of this battle reached Washington soon after he had left Philadelphia, and aroused in him confidence in the eventual success of the American cause.   He arrived in the vicinity of Boston on July second, and on the third took command of the troops drawn up on Cambridge common.

This army, though considerable in numbers and overflowing with patriotism, was lacking in military organization, and to the task of drilling and uniting it, and also supplying ammunition and further equipment, Washington applied himself through the summer and following winter, while maintaining a close siege over the British in Boston.   Early in March, 1776, under the cover of a bombardment from his base of operations, Washington secretly marched a large body of men to Dorchester Heights, a commanding position on the opposite side of Boston, and one of extreme menace to the British.   The latter awoke on the morning of March fifth, to find a repetition of the frowning embankments that had spurred them to action on Bunker Hill, this time on the landward side of the town, though separated from it by a small bay.

Realizing the seriousness of the situation, Howe made preparations for attack, but unfavorable weather prevailed for a day or two, giving the Americans opportunity for strengthening their position, and after some days of hesitation, the British evacuated Boston, sailing away on March seventeenth, and carrying with them about a thousand Tories, whom they

Boulder on Lexington Green

Bunker Hill

𝕺𝖑𝖉 𝕾𝖙𝖆𝖙𝖊 𝕳𝖔𝖚𝖘𝖊

𝕭𝖔𝖘𝖙𝖔𝖓

𝕸𝖆𝖘𝖘.

transported with their goods to Halifax. New England, the birthplace of the Revolution, was thus saved to the Americans, and freed, for the most part, from further strife in the barely awakened cause.

Washington, from time of taking command of the army, was the centre of interest, and the course of the Revolution was chiefly with the troops under his personal direction; but it is necessary, in even an outline of the war, to note certain secondary expeditions and lesser incidents in progress at the time when Washington was encamped before Boston.

Canada was recognized from the first, by the American leaders, as a menace to the unity of the colonies by reason of the possibilities it offered as a base for operations through the valley of the Hudson to the sea-coast, which would isolate New England and prevent its intercommunication, either offensive or defensive, with other sections. To obviate this danger, Washington early decided to attempt the conquest of Canada, and organized two expeditions, to travel different routes and meet at Quebec for a joint assault.

One under Montgomery passed up Lake Champlain and captured Montreal and intervening points. The other under Benedict Arnold embarked at Newburyport, and then, following the Kennebec River, and through the wilderness beyond, reached Quebec in December, 1775, after a journey of extraordinary difficulty and hardship. Montgomery, with but a remnant of his forces, soon arrived, and with those of Arnold — also greatly diminished — formed an attacking body of but little over a thousand men, to assault a city noted for its strong situation and elaborate fortifications. The attempt, though gallant and for a time encouraging, failed with the death of Montgomery and wounding of Arnold; and although held besieged by the latter for the rest of the winter, the city remained in the possession of the British, and in the spring the Americans were forced, by the approach of a powerful relief expedition under Sir Guy Carleton, to abandon their advantage and leave Canada for good and all.

At this time the British were using their ships, against which we could as yet oppose none, to harass outlying ports, and with apparently no plan other than the resulting terror and apprehension in all coast towns. Falmouth, Maine, now Portland, was bombarded and then burned; and the British, at the instigation of Lord Dunmore, Governor of the Province, attacked Hampton, Virginia, and later Norfolk. At both places they were repulsed, but Norfolk suffered heavily from bombardment and fire. Patriotism in the South was further stimulated by an attack on

𝕼𝖚𝖊𝖇𝖊𝖈 𝕰𝖝𝖕𝖊𝖉𝖎𝖙𝖎𝖔𝖓

Charleston, South Carolina, a few months later. A large fleet under Admiral Parker, with General Clinton for military commander, was organized to take that city and subdue the surrounding country ; news of this plan reached South Carolina, and active preparations were made to resist the invasion. Troops of militia, local and from neighboring states, occupied all available positions, and a fort of palmetto-wood was erected on Sullivan's Island and manned by five hundred men under Colonel Moultrie. This fort was the chief defense of the city and was relied upon to with- *1776* stand the brunt of the attack, although it was by some considered entirely inadequate for the purpose.

Early in June the British, in upwards of thirty vessels, arrived at the entrance to the harbor, but with characteristic delay, it was four weeks before they were ready to attack. Clinton's forces were rendered ineffective by being stupidly disembarked on a sand-bar from which they expected to cross to Sullivan's Island, but to which there was no practicable ford. Parker opened fire on Fort Sullivan with six ships, and after an engagement lasting all day, was obliged to withdraw what remained of his fleet and give up the attempt. It was a most notable victory for American courage and perseverance under almost overwhelming odds, and it raised Colonel Moultrie to a place among the greatest heroes of the war. An incident of this battle was the heroism of Sergeant Jasper in replanting on the bastion the colors which had been shot away.

As the evacuation of Boston had practically ended the war in New England, so the defeat at Charleston freed the South from further molestation for some years, and removed the centre of strife to the Middle States, where less determined resistance was to be feared. Washington, realizing that the British would turn to New York as their logical base of operations, removed his army to that place soon after the taking of Boston, and made preparations to defend the city as well as his inadequate and poorly equipped army might be able to. Congress, which had mainly directed its efforts to additional attempts to secure peaceful recognition from King George, had utterly failed, through inability or inattention, to provide for the increase or sustenance of the army, and was at any time liable to disruption from the growing differences of delegates as to the policy to be pursued. There was, as yet, no union, and therefore no responsible government which could organize internal affairs and collect funds. This condition, coupled with the vanishing of hope of any concession from the King, who had declared the colonists rebels and announced his determination to crush them, emphasized the need of a basis for a permanent government ; and after some hesitation on the part of representatives of a few states, *1776* it was voted, on the second of July, 1776, to announce to the world the principles for which the American people were contending. A committee, of which Thomas Jefferson, a delegate from Virginia, recently arrived, was chosen chairman, was appointed to formulate the declaration, the writing of which was entrusted to Jefferson. The result of his labor and the deliberations of the committee, was the Declaration of Independence, laid before Congress on the fourth of July and unanimously accepted.

Massachusetts

Charleston

Statue of Captain Nathan Hale by Macmonnies

This forceful and inspiring document attracted the attention of the civilized world, and made possible the union subsequently effected. It has maintained, and will ever hold, its position as the most revered and precious relic of American history ; and it is one of the evidences of the quality of mind and character which the early patriots brought to the cause of liberty.

From Philadelphia, where the people awaited breathlessly the peal of the State House bell, which should "Proclaim Liberty throughout all the land, to all the inhabitants thereof"; through New York, where the message was read to the troops drawn up on the Common, and was boisterously celebrated by the populace, which demonstrated its patriotism by tearing from the pedestal on Bowling Green an equestrian statue of George III, of gilded lead, that from glorifying the King was turned against him in the form of rebel bullets; to Boston, where, in some ways it meant more than it elsewhere could — the acceptance by the united colonies of the cause nurtured on Boston's wrongs — the country hailed with enthusiasm this brilliant crystalization by its ablest representatives, in solemn congress assembled, of the sentiments which for months had fired individuals everywhere, but had lacked the official approval of the leaders. A large measure of this unanimity was due to the widespread appreciation of Paine's "Common-Sense," published the previous winter, in which Thomas Paine, an Englishman who had been in this country but a short time, grasped and set forth in convincing style, the principles involved in the struggle with the mother country, and the reasons why rebellion was just and right. Paine showed the people what they sought and needed ; Congress declared it an accomplished fact and bestirred in its defense.

Meanwhile the cause in the field was experiencing misfortunes and disasters calculated to weaken its popularity, and was only saved from extermination by Washington's ability to successively extricate his army from seemingly overwhelming situations. He had established himself in New York and Brooklyn with the ten thousand troops that represented all that was available — many of that number for but a short period only — of the army brought from Boston, and endeavored to hold in check the large and powerful armies under Howe and Clinton, the latter having reached there from his defeat at Charleston, supported by powerful ships of war. His detachments on Long Island under Sullivan and Stirling were badly routed, and the situation there was strongly against him, when Washington brought over

New Hampshire

NEW HAMPSHIRE

Declaration of Independence

Old War Office, Lebanon Conn

reinforcements and engaged in preparing fortifications, as though intending a continuance of operations; but the next morning, August twenty-ninth, found the place utterly deserted, his army having been ferried across to New York under cover of the night and a beneficent fog. Colonel Glover's Marblehead fishermen accomplished this feat for Washington, and the British, who surrounded the Americans and expected an easy and decisive victory, were doomed to disappointment. They, however, knew their strength and Washington's weakness, and assailed him on all sides of the stand taken in New York, driving him in a few days to Harlem Heights. Washington's personal bravery as he rode among his panic-stricken men was the slender thread by which he was enabled to finally withdraw his troops.

It was especially desirable at this time that some knowledge be obtained of the intended movements of the British, and Washington accepted the services of Captain Nathan Hale of Connecticut, who volunteered to visit the enemy's camp as a spy. He penetrated the British lines and obtained the information without discovery, but on his way back was recognized and arrested by a Tory relative. He was taken before Howe and sentenced to death, and was executed September twenty-second. Every benefit of humanity and religion was denied him, yet he met his death with high courage, and his last words, "I only regret that I have but one life to give for my country," have become immortal.

In the face of his retreat, Washington sent detachments to check the advance of the enemy's outposts, and after sharp fighting drove them back to the main lines. The American position was here fairly strong, but not strong enough to warrant Washington in risking his army; so on the further advance of the British, he seized favorable points and held them in check until he could again retreat, this time to White Plains, on the bank of the Bronx River.

Once more the British under Howe thought to crush the American forces and end the war, and once more, after a sharp engagement, the Americans succeeded in escaping and establishing themselves in a stronger position at North Castle. Forts Washington and Lee, which defended the Hudson River at Harlem, were left garrisoned with the expectation of their being able to hold the position; but the British having obtained, through the treachery of a deserter from Fort Washington, complete information as to the strength and arrangement of that fortification, it was successfully assaulted on November sixteenth,

QUI TRANSTULIT SUSTINET

Connecticut

Captain
Nathan Hale

1776

**Carpenters Hall
Philadelphia Pa.**

and two thousand men taken prisoners. This loss, with General Lee's disobedience in withholding, on the other side of the Hudson, the large body of troops under his command, left Washington in a desperate situation. His army was reduced through these causes, and the expiration of the terms of enlistment of many of the militia, to the neighborhood of three thousand men, and continual discharges and desertions, with the failure of efforts to secure re-enlistments or fresh recruits, threatened to leave but a fraction of that number. Fortunately at this time General Lee's troops were brought in by General Sullivan, the former having been taken prisoner while at a distance from his army.

The British, holding all the important points captured, continued their advance to Trenton and occupied that place preparatory to marching on Philadelphia, but later abandoned that part of the plan. The fear of this disaster was intense in Philadelphia, and Congress considered it necessary to adjourn to Baltimore, after vesting the entire control of the war in Washington; a compliment which would have been more appreciated had it brought greater opportunities instead of adding to the perplexities of that general. He watched the enemy from a safe distance while exerting himself strenuously to strengthen his army, though with little success. The misfortunes which made the necessity most urgent operated against his efforts, and no enthusiasm could be aroused for an apparently failing cause. Little as the prospect offered, he realized that something must be done, and done quickly, or the new year would find him almost without men.

1776

Bold as the plan seemed when the possibilities were considered, Washington made up his mind to attack Trenton, and despatched several detachments to diverse points to ensure the surrounding of the enemy. Christmas night was the time settled upon for the assault, and Washington, with twenty-four hundred men, arrived at the bank of the Delaware in a fierce storm of snow and sleet, to find the river swollen and filled with swiftly-moving ice. To a lesser man the difficulties would have been insuperable, as they appeared to his aides, to whom the duty was intrusted of attacking from other points, and who failed to cross. To Washington it meant but the call

American Losses

for greater effort, and, encouraged by his example and guided by the hardy fishermen of Marblehead, the troops were safely, though with great difficulty, transported to the Trenton side, where they set out upon an exhausting march to the town, regardless of the storm and the pains of travel on the frozen ground. Colonel Rahl

NC NJ NY
SC V NE
G M P
UNITE OR DIE

1776

had been warned that Washington was planning an attack, but, as usual, affected to despise his opponent, and the twelve hundred Hessians were in the midst of a characteristic Christmas celebration from which all thought of the enemy was banished, when the foot-sore and wearied Americans burst upon them. Rahl's men, thoroughly panic-stricken, offered little or no resistance, and in attempting to rally them their commander was shot down. A few were killed and some escaped, but about one thousand, with all their artillery and stores, were made prisoners and taken in triumph to Philadelphia.

Washington lost no time, after this inspiring victory, in following up the advantage gained, and returning with fresh troops, re-occupied Trenton. Howe felt heavily the loss of prestige and men resulting from the defeat of Christmas night, and once more determined to overwhelm the meagre army of Washington and terminate the harassing rebellion. To this end Lord Cornwallis, with seven thousand men, set out from Princeton, January second. They were met on the road by detachments of Americans sent out to retard their movement, and slowly driving the skirmishers before them, made their way to Trenton.

The main body of the American army was entrenched just outside the town, on the further bank of the Assanpink, and here the British prepared to attack. An attempt to cross the bridge was repulsed, and Cornwallis contented himself for that day with cannonading the enemy from the opposite shore, and planning to assault them on the following morning when reinforced. The British habit of delay at critical junctures had before given Washington opportunity to extricate his army from dangerous situations, and he took advantage of it on this occasion to abandon his position on the Assanpink and march on Princeton — where Cornwallis had left three regiments of his army — from whence he hoped to pass to Brunswick and capture the large quantity of British stores known to be there. With his usual adroitness, Washington withdrew undetected by the army on the opposite bank, which regarded the brightly burning camp-fires, kindled for the purpose, as undoubted evidence of the continued presence of the Americans. Princeton was reached early on the morning of January third, and the British troops were encountered just as they were leaving to join

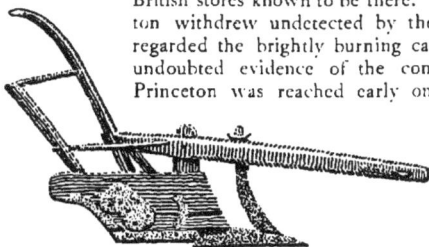

General Putnam's Plough

1777

Trenton

1777

Old Mill Newport R. I.

Cornwallis. A battle ensued, which, though at times apparently in favor of the British—owing to the inability of the Americans, through lack of equipment, to meet bayonet charges—resulted finally in a splendid victory for Washington, whose personal valor and encouragement strengthened his men and turned the balance to his side. The British fled to Brunswick, but the day was so far spent that Washington deemed it unwise to attack that place, and after destroying the bridges between his army and that of Cornwallis, withdrew to Somerset Court House, and thence to Morristown, where he went into winter quarters. Cornwallis, discomfited at his failure at Trenton and the defeat of his troops at Princeton, returned to Brunswick to protect his magazines, and suspended operations for the winter.

The effect of these victories on the country and the outside world was to raise the American cause from the lowest ebb of discouragement to enthusiastic support at home and increased respect abroad. France, though yet unwilling to openly favor this country, was secretly sending supplies, and from that country and Germany and Prussia came able and devoted officers to assist our cause. Recruiting became easier and re-

1777 enlistments frequent, enabling Washington to greatly strengthen his army and prepare for a renewal of the struggle with the coming of spring.

Events moved slowly at this time, a condition to which the American cause in the field was frequently indebted, and yet the forces at work were making for results soon to place the struggle for independence on a basis of international recognition and eventual support. After declaring independence, Congress had dispatched emissaries to the courts of Europe, and especially to France, where the sympathy of progressive leaders established the cause in substantial favor. Many of the ablest members were thus employed, or were called to their homes to direct the sustaining operations of the war, so that the representation left was appreciably inferior as a whole, and of little real assistance as an executive body. It was inadequate to the task of supporting the army or of adding materially to its numbers, and its financial system, lacking bassi and credit, was a failure from the start. To the army it commissioned officers in many cases incompetent; and through a misunderstanding of facts, or unduly influenced by

Rhode Island

Washington's Headquarters Newburgh N. Y.

interested parties, it superseded competent generals at critical times and placed inferior men in command. Lacking official support, the Revolution was sustained by popular contribution through the state leaders, the work of Robert Morris, of Philadelphia, being especially memorable, and of inestimable service to Washington in his efforts to hold together and strengthen his army.

Connecticut bore a generous share in equipping and sustaining the troops, and at this time suffered locally from the proximity of the British quartered at New York. On April twenty-sixth, 1777, Governor Tryon of New York, with two thousand British and Tories, attacked and burned Danbury, and destroyed a large quantity of American stores. On the following day the militia, under Generals Wooster, Arnold, ₁₋₋₋ and Silliman, forced Tryon to the coast after an engagement at Ridgefield, and the British embarked under heavy fire. General Wooster, a veteran of seventy years, was mortally wounded. A month later the Americans under Colonel Meigs retaliated by crossing from Connecticut to Sag Harbor, on Long Island, where they burned twelve British vessels and destroyed stores, bringing back ninety prisoners without the loss of a man.

Another incident illustrative of the daring and adroitness of the American soldiers was the capture of General Prescott, commander of the British forces in the neighborhood of Rhode Island, whose tyranny had excited the indignation of the people. On the night of July tenth, Lieutenant Barton of Providence, with forty men, stealthily approached Prescott's headquarters by water, and, overpowering the sentinel, secured Prescott, who was in bed, and escaped before the alarm spread to the troops.

Raids in Connecticut

Kingston N.Y.
Van Steenburg House

1777

Congress recognized this act by promoting Barton to the rank of colonel and presenting him a sword.

Spring brought a renewal of activity in the armies facing each other in the South, and in the North it saw the development of a plan to effect the separation of New England from the other states. This had long been recognized as an impending possibility, and the division of the North under General Schuyler, though weak in numbers, was so placed as to offer the utmost resistance to the anticipated movement. Lake Champlain, the natural path of such invasion, had, the previous summer, been the scene of a strenuous, if not mighty, struggle with the same object, when Benedict Arnold had, by dint of extraordinary effort, created a flotilla, effectively armed and manned, with which he vigorously contested Sir Guy Carleton's ascent of the lake ; and, while ultimately forced to retreat, so delayed and crippled the enemy that the British expedition was fruitless for that season, so far as the main object was concerned. The ground thus gained was held, and served Sir John Burgoyne, the successor of Carleton, to launch with great pomp in June, 1777, an army of eight thousand men, including Indians — now for the first time employed — which maintained its triumphant progress only so long as the waters of the lake formed the line of passage. They erected fortifications on Mt. Defiance, near Ticonderoga, from which commanding position they were able to throw a destructive fire into the fort ; and General St. Clair, who occupied the post with somewhat less than three thousand ill-armed troops, abandoned it on the night of July fifth, and undertook to join Schuyler at Fort Edward. The British started after him and several times engaged his rear guard, but at the end of a week the Americans succeeded in reaching Schuyler, though with the loss of some men and a considerable amount of baggage, captured by the British at Skenesboro. At this point the struggle with natural conditions began, which offered, difficult as it was, the only means by which Burgoyne could pass to Albany, where he hoped to meet forces under Howe, which were to come up the Hudson and thus dominate the line from Canada to Long Island. Schuyler, realizing the overwhelming force of the invading army, fell back in slow retreat, destroying the only road as he passed, burning bridges and clogging streams, besides devastating the country of everything that could be utilized to sustain an army. Under these circumstances Burgoyne's progress, with all the facilities of a thoroughly equipped army, was only about one mile a day, and the Americans were enabled to

Burgoyne's Expedition

keep well out of reach until reinforcements and a favorable situation should enable them to make a stand.

A strong detachment of the invaders, under St. Leger, had been sent to the westward to take Fort Stanwix, held by General Ganesvoort. They met with determined resistance, and vigorous fighting took place at the fort, and at Oriskany, where *1777* General Herkimer, who had come to the relief of Ganesvoort with a large following of frontiersmen, fell into an ambush of the enemy. The brave general was mortally wounded early in the engagement, but with great fortitude continued to direct the battle and succeeded in routing the British, who, however, continued to maintain the siege. After some weeks ineffectually spent, they were frightened into a precipitate retreat by news of the approach of Arnold with reinforcements, and made their way to Canada, minus everything that tended to impede flight.

Burgoyne, experiencing to the full the difficulties imposed by Schuyler, felt the need of provisions, and detached a party of six hundred, under Colonel Baum, to raid the country in what is now Vermont, and capture stores held at Bennington. This party was met near Bennington by the farmers, who had hastily gathered under General Stark, and defeated with the loss of their baggage and artillery. Another party of equal numbers which had been sent out a few days afterward to reinforce the first, came up a few hours later and suffered like defeat. More than half the British were taken prisoners, and upwards of two hundred killed, leaving but a third to make its way back to the main army. These misfortunes were rapidly bringing Burgoyne to a realization of the doubtfulness of final success, which success would have appeared still more remote could he have known, as he did later, that Howe's orders had been so delayed that no help could reach him from that quarter in season to avail.

The American victories at Oriskany and Bennington spread confidence throughout the country, and troops gathered to the support of the northern army, which Congress, with great injustice to Schuyler, now placed under the command of General Horatio Gates, a soldier much inferior to the former in ability and attainments. Gates reaped the benefit of all the hard work done by Schuyler, and entered upon his command under most favorable conditions. Burgoyne, pressed for supplies and threatened in his rear by General Lincoln—who with two thousand troops was even then retaking Ticonderoga—was on the downward slope of effectiveness, while the American army was constantly receiving reinforcements, — among which were Morgan's Virginia riflemen sent by Washington, — and with Arnold returned from Fort Stanwix, was daily gaining strength and courage, and numbered about three thousand men to thirty-five hundred of the British. Gates, after a delay of several *1777* weeks, established himself at Bemis Heights, on the west bank of the Hudson, and awaited the enemy. They arrived on September nineteenth, and on the following day attacked the Americans in their full strength. Gates proved utterly inefficient, watching the battle from the rear without taking part in it, and the conduct of the fight devolved upon the regimental commanders, among whom Arnold was the dominant figure. The battle continued until dark-

New York

𝔅𝔢𝔫𝔫𝔦𝔫𝔤𝔱𝔬𝔫

Old Senate House
Kingston N. Y.

1777

ness, when the Americans drew off to their intrenchments, leaving the British in possession of their ground, but suffering from a severe repulse, their loss being double that of the Continentals.

This was the beginning of the end with Burgoyne. On October seventh he made another attempt to break the American lines, taking fifteen hundred of his best troops; but his columns were stubbornly met, and finally, with Morgan, Dearborn, and Arnold leading, the Americans routed the British and drove them to their intrenched camp, where the fighting was continued until stopped by darkness. Arnold was on the field without authority, he having been deprived of his command by Gates, but was unable to restrain his ardor, and placed himself at the head of his old division, which he inspired to brilliant service; he was badly wounded in the later attack.

The British were now in a desperate situation; beaten and hopeless of reinforcement they sought to retreat through Saratoga, but found themselves surrounded by the gathering Americans, and a few days later Burgoyne gave up the attempt and opened negotiations for surrender. The document was signed October sixteenth, and by it an army of nearly six thousand, with all equipments, was turned over to Gates, and the long-cherished plan to control the line from Canada to the mouth of the Hudson came finally to naught. Clinton, in pursuance of belated orders, had started to Burgoyne's assistance, but his enthusiasm waned after capturing Forts Montgomery and Clinton, and contenting himself with sending a detachment to raid Kingston, which was burned October thirteenth, he returned to New York, leaving the North, when rid of Burgoyne, in undisputed possession of the Americans. News of this triumph was of inestimable help to the American cause in Europe, and created a prestige that made possible the French Alliance.

Washington, though not active in this northern campaign, was none the less a factor in its success, as his watchfulness and employment of Howe and his army in the Middle South was largely for the purpose of maintaining the separation of the British forces, which he knew to be essential to American victory on the Hudson. While Burgoyne was embarking, with so much éclat, his ill-fated expedition, Washington, who had removed from his winter quarters at Morristown, New Jersey, to Middlebrook, was endeavoring to check Howe's advance without hazarding his small army in open battle. Howe, tiring of these tactics, returned to New York, where,

1777

New Jersey

Saratoga

Monument to André's capture
Tarrytown N.Y.

on July twenty-third, he embarked eighteen thousand men with a view of reaching Philadelphia by water. Washington discovered his motive and immediately marched his troops to that place, hoping to reassure the people before engaging the enemy. His army in point of effectiveness numbered about ten thousand, though in actual numbers several thousand more, and among his officers was the Marquis de Lafayette, a young French nobleman, who, filled with sympathy and enthusiasm for the cause of the colonies, had, in spite of the disapproval of his king, reached this country with Baron de Kalb, a German veteran, and was by Congress commissioned Major-General. Lafayette endeared himself to Washington and to the army, and became, next to Washington, one of the most prominent figures in the war.

Howe, finding the Delaware fortified against him, entered Chesapeake Bay and landed his army at Elkton, Maryland, about fifty miles from Philadelphia. From this point he marched toward the city, reaching Chad's Ford, on the Brandywine — where the Americans were encamped — September eleventh. The resulting battle was disastrous to the patriots, and although well planned and bravely fought, ended at night in their retreat to Chester, and later to the neighborhood of Philadelphia. Count Pulaski, a Polish volunteer, distinguished himself in this action and was subsequently commissioned Brigadier General by Congress, in recognition of his gallantry.

Washington, though defeated, still hoped to keep the British from Philadelphia, and prepared to engage them again near Goshen, but was prevented by a severe storm, and was then forced to withdraw to Reading to protect his stores, which were threatened by the enemy. He left General Wayne with fifteen hundred men to check the advance on Philadelphia, but the latter was surprised by a midnight attack and driven back with considerable loss, leaving the city open to the invaders, who

Liberty Bell

1777

entered September twenty-sixth. Fearing this result, Congress had removed, some days before, to Lancaster, from which a few days later it moved to York, where it remained during the British occupancy of the capital.

The danger to Reading having passed, Washington resolved on another attack, and with two thousand five hundred reinforcements he engaged the British troops stationed at Germantown, near Philadelphia; but through the failure of militia on which he relied, the effort was defeated after a severe struggle, in which the American loss was heavy. Forts Mifflin and Mercer, the former on Mud Island, in the Delaware, and the latter at Red Bank, New Jersey, were still held by the Americans, who had established them to protect Philadelphia from naval attack. These the British assaulted with the aid of the fleet from Chesapeake Bay, and after a determined but hopeless resistance the Americans were forced to evacuate, November eighteenth, leaving the harbor unobstructed for the passage of British ships. To close a season disastrous in its immediate results, Washington, early in December, went into winter quarters at Valley Forge, on the Schuylkill, and struggled to maintain the organization of his army under conditions which would have been insurmountable to another general, or with an army striving for a lesser end.

1717

The cause of independence experienced its darkest days in that memorable camp. Thousands of men were unable to leave the rude huts they had built for shelter, for lack of clothing to cover them; they were reduced to the barest extremity for food, and yet their patriotism and faith in their commander triumphed over these miseries and sustained them until spring, when a turn of fortune brought once more the necessaries of life and comfortable equipment. During the long winter, Washington suffered not only the anguish of sympathy for his starving troops, but from the machinations of envious and disgruntled subordinates, and the criticism of some of the leaders in Congress. It was hoped, by a considerable faction, to supersede Washington by Gates — the latter's victory over Burgoyne being contrasted with Washington's campaign about Philadelphia — and sufficient support was obtained to secure control of the Board of War, which, with Gates at the head, was a source of annoyance and affront to Washington, while it utterly failed in its duties of providing for the army.

Delaware

Valley Forge

While these conditions existed at the seat of war, forces were elsewhere working for speedy and permanent improvement. The King of France, overborne by his ministers, had signed early in February a treaty of alliance and commerce, acknowledging the independence of the American Colonies. This meant money and ships and ready supplies, besides establishing the United States on a recognized footing at the capitals of Europe. The victory at Saratoga, which had encouraged France to this action, had startled England into a belated concession of privileges, which a peace commission was sent over to propose; but the time for such measures was past and they were rejected by Congress, which declared that no proposals would be entertained except on a basis of complete independence and the withdrawal of British troops. This, of course, was not contemplated, and the commission ingloriously returned. The action of France was regarded by England as a declaration of war, and preparations were made for strengthening the situation of the troops in America. General Howe, who, it was realized, had done nothing more than seize upon comfortable winter quarters for his army, was recalled and superseded by General Clinton. Philadelphia being of no military value to the British without a line of communication with the main army at New York, it was decided to abandon it ere the French fleet could come to the assistance of Washington's army and force the evacuation. In pursuance of these orders Clinton, who had assumed command the latter part of May, so hastened preparations that on June eighteenth he left the city and started his army across New Jersey.

Washington, whose patience and endurance the winter had so severely tried, was now well equipped, thanks to the efforts of Greene, who in March, as quartermaster-general, succeeded the incompetent Board of War; the spring levies had filled his ranks, and best of all, his army, which had been drilled all winter by Baron Steuben — a distinguished Prussian officer — was now for the first time in perfect training. Under such gratifying conditions it is not strange that Washington wished to intercept Clinton and match his strength against the British; but a council of his officers by their disapproval so delayed him, that, though he finally overruled their decision, Clinton was then so far advanced that to overtake him required extraordinary effort, and forced the troops to a fatiguing march, which at the last became so hurried that many threw away their knap-

Fort Pitt
Pittsburg Pa.

The French Alliance

𝔅𝔢𝔱𝔱𝔶 𝔚𝔬𝔰𝔰 𝔥𝔬𝔲𝔰𝔢
𝔓𝔥𝔦𝔩𝔞𝔡𝔢𝔩𝔭𝔥𝔦𝔞,
𝔴𝔥𝔢𝔯𝔢 𝔣𝔦𝔯𝔰𝔱 𝔄𝔪𝔢𝔯𝔦=
𝔠𝔞𝔫 𝔣𝔩𝔞𝔤 𝔴𝔞𝔰 𝔪𝔞𝔡𝔢

sacks in their desire to reach the enemy. The British were advised of Washington's approach, and though numbering seventeen thousand, were headed for the coast by the most direct route, their march fast becoming flight under the vexations of climate and the harassing attacks of the New Jersey militia. On the twenty-sixth of June they encamped at Monmouth Court House with Washington but a few miles behind, and a detachment under Lee, which had been sent in advance, within striking distance. The latter, Washington ordered to attack as soon as the enemy should resume the march in the morning, promising support as soon as he could come up. Lee, an Englishman who had been a source of trouble to Washington all through the war, was impressed with Clinton's invincibility, and fearing to engage him, contented himself with unimportant manœuvers, until Clinton, seeing his opportunity, charged, and had started the Americans in retreat when Washington, whom the incredible news found straining every nerve to reach the field of battle, galloped on the scene, and overcome with rage, demanded of Lee an explanation of his course. This Lee was unable to give, and ordering him to the rear, where the next day he was court-martialed and suspended from his command, Washington rallied the troops, that had failed wholly from the lack of efficient ordering, and with the arrival of the main army recovered the ground and drove the British in retreat. Under the cover of the night the retreat was kept up, and Clinton succeeded in reaching the coast and embarking before the Americans could again come up with him. His army was reduced by two thousand, in the march and battle, and had it not been for the incompetence of Lee, would have been utterly destroyed. As it was, he was beaten, and the campaign which Washington had lost at Brandywine and Germantown, was redeemed at Monmouth. An incident of this battle was the bravery of Molly Pitcher, the wife of an American artilleryman. She was bringing water to her husband when she saw him fall, and heard an order for withdrawing his gun; determined that it should not be silenced, she took his place and served the gun throughout the fight. In recognition of her patriotism Washington appointed her a sergeant in the army, where she became widely known and popular.

During the summer of 1778 the war made little progress, so far as the main armies were concerned. The British were now confined to New York, with an out-

𝔐𝔬𝔫𝔪𝔬𝔲𝔱𝔥

Independence Hall Philadelphia

post at Newport, Rhode Island, and evinced little inclination for aggressive measures. Early in July the French fleet, under Count d'Estaing, appeared off Sandy Hook, but owing to their greater draught were unable to approach the British fleet. In lieu of this, a plan was arranged for destroying, in conjunction with a land force, the British garrison and ships at Newport. D'Estaing arrived there with his fleet August eighth, and his presence with the forces under Sullivan, Greene, and Lafayette caused the British to destroy their men-of-war and other vessels in the harbor. While preparations for the attack were being made, a British squadron appeared, and the French went outside to engage it, but a very severe storm arose and scattered the fleets, injuring the vessels so that the British were forced to return to New York, and the French went to Boston, to refit. Upon this the land forces, which also suffered from the storm, were obliged to withdraw without accomplishing their purpose, though a sharp engagement took place between four thousand reinforcements, which Clinton had brought from New York, and a division under Green, in which the British were repulsed. Clinton occupied himself in ravaging the surrounding country and burning shipping at New Bedford, returning to New York soon afterward and subsequently abandoning Newport.

One of the particularly disturbing features of the summer were the Indian raids, made at the instigation of British agents and participated in by many Tories. Wyoming, Pennsylvania, and Cherry Valley, New York, suffered frightfully in this way, hundreds of men, women, and children falling victims to the tomahawk, while in many instances the torture was much more severe. Further west the British had seized old French trading posts and garrisoned them with regulars and Indians, to ensure the unlimited extension of British territory when the victory should be won. They also sought to uproot the settlement in what is now Kentucky, but were tenaciously resisted by the hardy pioneers under the lead of Boone, Logan, Kenton, and other intrepid woodsmen.

Among these was one who realized the value of the outposts that the British had seized, and determined that the vast territory dominated by them should be held by Americans. Kaskaskia, Vincennes, and Cahokia, in the Illinois country, were the

Pennsylvania

Newport

Chew Mansion Germantown Pa.

coveted settlements, and George Rogers Clark, a native of Virginia, the far-seeing frontiersman who set out to take them with less than two hundred men, raised by his personal efforts under the authority of Governor Patrick Henry of Virginia. Overcoming all obstacles, they reached Kaskaskia on the evening of July fourth, and Clark by skillful manœuvers took the garrison completely by surprise, and overpowering the guards, compelled the surrender of forces two or three times greater in number than his own. Vincennes and Cahokia followed with little trouble, but the difficulty was to hold the posts with his small following, of which many of the men were anxious to return to their homes. At this time the British arrived with a strong force and retook Vincennes, but owing to the lateness of the season hesitated about attacking Kaskaskia, held by Clark with the main body of his command. Neither the season nor the condition of the country had any terrors for Clark, and getting together one hundred and seventy men who could be depended upon, they started for Vincennes early in February, undertaking fearlessly a journey of over two hundred miles, in which they experienced hardships of every kind, including hunger, and a march through miles of icy water, waist high, but, in spite of these, arrived at their destination on the twenty-second of the month, and after a short fight forced the fort to again surrender.

The importance of this exploit was far-reaching, as it not only secured to the United States vast territory in the West, but it broke, from that time, the alliance with the Indians, which the British had created with difficulty, and upon which they largely depended.

The British, from their only stronghold, New York, kept up their devastating raids on the surrounding country, descending early in September on Buzzards Bay, where they destroyed shipping and privateers to the number of seventy sail, continu-

Major Clark's Expedition

ing through New Bedford and Fairhaven the pillage and destruction, and finally returning to New York with a large number of cattle and sheep captured at Martha's Vineyard. On the thirtieth of the same month they sailed to Little Egg Harbor, New Jersey, where they captured a considerable quantity of American stores.

This employment of his army, while perhaps a degree more creditable than absolute inaction, would never win for Clinton the control of America; and having tried and failed in successive attempts to hold the Northern and Middle States, the British turned again to the South, as offering the only remaining opportunity for lasting victory. Driven out of Boston, defeated and destroyed on the Hudson, balked at Philadelphia, and menaced at New York, they with some reasonableness hoped, by gaining a foothold in a thinly populated country, where loyalism was undoubtedly stronger, to extend operations on a permanent basis until they could unite with the Northern forces. The South, unmolested since Clinton and Parker's inglorious attack on Charleston, was unprepared for resistance and was divided by party differences that under the strain of war developed into serious civil conflict.

To this promising field, then, Clinton turned his attention, with immediate results that seemed to fully justify his deductions, and warranted confidence in the success of his ultimate plan. A partially successful raid under General Provost came out of Florida and pillaged the coast towns of Georgia, but the first important move was against Savannah. On the twenty-ninth of December, Colonel Campbell landed with an army of three thousand and attacked the city, which was defended by General Robert Howe with less than a thousand men, and those without experience in action. The British were easily victorious, and completely scattered the opposing force, taking some five hundred prisoners and capturing valuable stores. Following this, Provost returned and captured Sunbury, which had repulsed his first raid, and Campbell with a division of his troops advanced successfully on Augusta. Thus Georgia, the last to renounce the royal authority, was the first to again feel its yoke, the British being now in virtual possession of the State.

General Benjamin Lincoln was sent by Congress to command the Southern department, but met with little success. He succeeded in raising a small army, but attempting prematurely to recover Augusta and Savannah, his force was seriously reduced without the attainment of his object, and he was obliged to retire to the hills

White Hall

Anne Arundel Co. Maryland

The War in the South

with but a handful of men, leaving the British in full possession of Georgia. The direct results of his campaign were the gallant repulse of the British at Fort Royal by General Moultrie, the defeat and dispersal at Kettle Creek of a band of seven hundred Tories under Colonel Boyd, who was shot in the engagement, and the preservation of Charleston, which Provost had set out to attack, but from which he was compelled by Lincoln's advance to withdraw.

Encouraged by their progress in the South, the British resumed with greater boldness their periodic raids in the North. Under Sir George Collier and General

Arnold Mansion Philadelphia

Matthews they entered Hampton Roads, May ninth, ravaging Norfolk and Portsmouth, and then sailed for New York, where they assisted Clinton in capturing the unfinished fortifications at Stony Point, by which the Americans had hoped to control King's Ferry. An expedition had been sent against West Greenwich, Connecticut, the previous March, which is memorable chiefly on account of General Putnam's bold escape from what seemed certain capture. He had rallied a company to oppose the British, who were on their way to destroy the salt-works at Horse Neck, but was unable to offer effective resistance to the fifteen hundred invaders, and his men were soon dispersed. Putnam sought to reach Stamford, but was pursued by the British, who were fast gaining on him, when he turned his horse over the edge of a steep, rocky bluff and rode safely to the bottom, leaving his astonished pursuers

General Putnam's Ride

daunted and baffled at the top. Another expedition, under Governor Tryon, left New York for Connecticut early in July, and sailing along the coast plundered New Haven, East Haven, Fairfield and Norwalk, which latter place was also burned.

These measures were met by the Americans with movements against Stony Point and Verplank's Point, and later against the British garrison at Paulus Hook. These were not wholly retaliatory, as Washington feared from the capture of Stony Point the extension of British occupation through a series of such posts, which would accomplish all that was striven for in Burgoyne's campaign, and cut off his army and the Southern states from the recruits and supplies so generously furnished by New England. He therefore determined to retake the fort at once, and entrusted the work to General Wayne, one of his most intrepid aids. General Wayne with a few hundred men reached the precipitous slopes in the rear of the fort on the evening of July sixteenth, and in a dashing assault, upon which the heavy fire of the garrison made no impression, they mounted the breast-works and compelled a speedy surrender. Nearly five hundred prisoners were taken, and guns and munitions of great value captured. After training the guns of the fort on Verplank's Point, opposite, and compelling its evacuation, the Americans leveled the works and returned to the main army. Their achievement is looked upon as one of the most brilliant of the war.

Paulus Hook, now the site of a part of Jersey City, was one of the strongest natural positions held by the British; nearly surrounded by water, it was approachable only by the post road, of which it originally formed the terminus and landing place of the ferry from New York. Major Harry Lee undertook the capture, and surprised it early on the morning of August nineteenth. The British had little time for resistance before they were overpowered by the attacking party, which secured upwards of one hundred and fifty prisoners — a number greater than that of the Americans — and quickly withdrew, lest the alarm spread to the main body of the enemy and retreat be cut off.

Another undertaking, though carefully planned

1770

Doorway Harwood House Annapolis

Maryland

Stony Point

Mount Vernon

1779

and fitted out at great expense, met with disaster and utterly failed. This was the expedition against the British post at Castine, near the mouth of the Penobscot River, organized in Massachusetts, in which thirty-seven vessels were engaged, and had entered the river, when, on August thirteenth, they were hemmed in by a British fleet of superior force which suddenly appeared. The Americans, rather than see their ships fall into the hands of the British, beached and burned them, making their way back to Boston overland.

The American navy, from the poverty of national resources an inconsiderable power heretofore, received at this time a memorable accession in the fleet under John Paul Jones, fitted out at L'Orient, France, by the American and French governments. Jones, by birth a Scotchman, had already shown high ability in the service of America, and when, after many tedious disappointments, he found himself in command of an effective if not powerful fleet, he lost no time in making his presence felt among the shipping of Great Britain. He intercepted and captured many merchant vessels, in some cases boldly entering harbors to destroy them, and spread terror of his name throughout the British Isles. These exploits, while of importance in a scheme of warfare, were far from sufficient to the aggressive character of Jones, and he eagerly sought an encounter with armed vessels, though the conditions might apparently be against him. Such an opportunity came to him off Flamborough Head, September twenty-third, when he overtook two British ships of war, the Serapis and Countess of Scarborough, convoying a large fleet of merchantmen. Jones commanded the Bonhomme Richard, his flagship, and had with him but two other vessels of his squadron, the Alliance and Pallas, the others having been lost sight of in a gale. The British ships were greatly superior in size and armament, the Serapis being the larger, and a much newer and stouter vessel than the Bonhomme Richard, with which she engaged. The Countess of Scarborough soon struck to her opponents, the Alliance and Pallas, and the three remained in a group apart, leaving the two larger vessels to struggle for mastery. The battle that ensued is renowned in history as an example of the triumph of personal invincibility in the face of apparent ruin.

1779

The Bonhomme Richard and the Serapis fought at close range until both were badly battered and pierced, and then, grappled together, the guns of each touching the other's side, they continued their fearful work of carnage and destruction. On several occasions the Richard

Washington's Coat of Arms

Commodore John Paul Jones

was reported to be sinking, but by extraordinary effort was kept afloat, and at last Pearson, the captain of the Serapis, yielded to his antagonist at a moment when, as far as material evidence was credible, the victory might well have been his own. The Alliance, which should have helped the Richard, remained

Mount Vernon

1779

aloof during the greater part of the engagement, and when at last she came up, nearly ruined Jones's chance by firing broadsides which swept the deck of the Richard. This action was excused on the ground of mistaken identity, but Landais' jealousy of Jones and his restiveness under the latter's superior authority, give color to a presumption of traitorous intent, and he was soon afterwards dismissed from the navy. The prizes were taken to Holland, and Jones, after a short stay in Paris, where his achievement was enthusiastically honored, returned to America, and received the thanks of Congress for his eminent services.

While Jones was receiving his vessels from France, the French fleet under D'Estaing, which had been cruising in West Indian waters, suddenly returned to the coast and captured four British men-of-war at Savannah. The French commander resolved to follow up this victory by recovering the town, and sought the help of the militia in the undertaking. Several weeks elapsed before the South Carolinians with Lincoln, who came to their aid, could complete an effective organization, and in this time the British had received reinforcements and erected formidable defences. D'Estaing, chafing under the delay, demanded an immediate attack, and on October ninth, the allies gallantly assaulted the works and succeeded in planting the flags of America and France on the ramparts, but they could not maintain their position, and finally were repulsed with great loss. The brave Pulaski was killed in this action, as was Sergeant Jasper, the hero of Fort Moultrie; and Count d'Estaing, who led his troops in person, was severely wounded. The French fleet put to sea, and Lincoln, with about two thousand men, withdrew to Charleston, where the people, desirous of protection, urged them to remain.

The British, encouraged by their victory, appeared off the coast of Georgia early in 1780 with a fleet under Admiral Arbuthnot, bringing Clinton and eight thousand *1780* men, who were placed in commanding positions about Charleston, where they were joined by Cornwallis with troops to the number of three thousand. General Lincoln, who had remained in the city, had been reinforced by a considerable body

**Tool House
Mount Vernon**

of Virginia veterans, but his forces could offer no effective resistance to an army numbering four to his one. Aided by the fleet, which ran Fort Moultrie without difficulty, the British instituted an aggressive siege which resulted in the capitulation of the city on May twelfth; General Lincoln and all his men were taken prisoners.

With the loss of the last remnant of Lincoln's army, organized defense was obliterated in the South. The British spread over and devastated South Carolina as they did before in Georgia, plundering all not avowedly loyal, and committing outrages calculated to embitter the patriots and strengthen them in their later resistance.

A detachment of two thousand men under DeKalb had been sent South to augment the forces there, and this was now utilized as a nucleus of a new army. As many more were soon added by enlistment and the accession of isolated bands, and Gates, in whom Congress had great confidence, based on a misconception of his part in the capture of Burgoyne, was sent, against the judgment of Washington, to take command. Under conservative leadership this army would have grown and developed into an effective force, but without waiting for these processes, and apparently without consideration of its weakness, Gates led it to Camden, then an important center for the British. The despair resulting from the loss of Savannah and Charleston had been broken by minor though brilliant successes at Fishing Creek and Hanging Rock, and the patriots rallying under Marion, Sumter, and Pickens were harassing the British with a partisan warfare destructive of their sense of security, though lacking in effective organization. These leaders joined forces with Gates; but they added nothing to the strength of the attack on Camden, as both Marion and Sumter were detached for special operations, the latter taking four hundred of the best troops in addition to his own.

The British under Lord Rawdon, knowing of Gates' advance, set out to intercept and surprise him, and on August sixteenth, the armies came suddenly together, neither being aware of the proximity of the other. A battle was immediately ordered, and a line of militia, never before under fire, was marched in the first charge against the perfectly drilled regulars of the British. The natural result was, that the Americans, frightened by the solid fire of the enemy, broke and fled, leaving to DeKalb and his Continentals the whole burden of resistance. The latter fought with remarkable cour-

Virginia

**General Gates
in the South**

age, but they were hopelessly outnumbered, and, after losing eight hundred men, including DeKalb, were obliged to retreat and save themselves as best they could. Sumter's detachment, which had captured the British wagon train, was overtaken by Tarleton and routed with the loss of half its men, killed or captured. The re-formed southern army, barely started in its mission, was thus effectually scattered, and once more the British were free to extend their lines and prosecute their plan of northward conquest.

Old Entrance Mount Vernon

This immunity was of short duration, however, the rigorous measures adopted by Cornwallis quickly bearing fruit in an uprising fatal to British supremacy. Wishing to free himself from the annoyance of local attacks, Cornwallis sent a division under Colonel Ferguson to range the western borders of the Carolinas and intimidate the inhabitants. The threats of the invaders roused the mountaineers, who had hitherto contented themselves with repressing Indian aggression, and gathering under favorite leaders, they assembled on the Watuga, late in September, to the number of nearly twelve hundred. They chose Colonel Campbell — leader of the Virginians — chief commander, and under his direction were more closely united and instructed in methods of attack. They were later joined by upwards of three hundred from North Carolina, and started to crush the detachment under Ferguson. The British commander had word of their coming, and undertook to elude them ; but being unsuccessful in this, took up a strong position on Kings' Mountain and awaited the conflict. To shorten the pursuit the backwoodsmen had divided their force, the pick of men and horses to the number of seven hundred entering on a forced march, leaving the rest to come up as they could. Riding night and day in their impatience to attain their object, the Americans arrived in the vicinity of the British camp on the morning of October seventh, and immediately arranged the attack. The British had more men, and a strong position on the top of a wooded hill ; but every man in the attacking force was a trained Indian fighter and thoroughly at home in such a situation. They charged from opposite sides of the hill, and a repulse on one side was immediately followed by an assault on the other, thus keeping the British in constant motion, and gradually reducing the intervening space, until arriving at the top they surrounded and overpowered the enemy, forcing unconditional surrender. Ferguson and fully one-third of his men were killed, and the victors secured a large store of arms and ammunition, the lack of which was everywhere a serious hindrance to the struggling patriots.

King's Mountain

𝔆𝔩𝔞𝔤𝔢𝔱𝔱'𝔰 𝔗𝔞𝔟𝔢𝔯𝔫 𝔄𝔩𝔢𝔵𝔞𝔫𝔡𝔯𝔦𝔞 𝔙𝔞.

The tide of war thus ebbing and flowing, rose perceptibly for the Americans from this time, the people, encouraged by the destruction of the merciless foe that dominated the frontier, rising in scattered bands to pick off isolated British posts and even driving the main army to seek security nearer the sea-coast. Marion and Sumter appeared in unexpected quarters, cutting off supplies and routing loyalist militia, leading Tarleton hither and thither in futile attempts to reach them. He finally came up with Sumter at Blackstocks and was severely repulsed. The British, once more on the defensive, were checked in their northward march, and all that was needed to permanently cripple them was an organized army to which the roving bands could rally. This Congress undertook, for the third time, to supply ; but depleted ranks and bankrupt finances were conditions not lightly subjected, and Greene, whom Washington was privileged to appoint to this command, could obtain but little in material equipment, either of men or outfittings, and was obliged to depend on appeals to the Southern States, backed by recommendations of the central government. In some aspects Greene's expedition was in the nature of a forlorn hope. Two armies had been sacrificed in the same cause, exhausting the resources of the northern division, which could now spare but a mere body-guard to the departing general. Disaffection was rife in the Continental army on account of the worthlessness of the currency with which it was paid, and enlistments were correspondingly difficult to obtain. In the face of this discouraging outlook Greene went resolutely to his task, rousing the country as he traveled through it and importuning the governors for aid of any kind. His energetic measures brought him some immediate assistance, and more followed as he journeyed South, leaving a train of activity where apathy had

𝔊𝔢𝔫𝔢𝔯𝔞𝔩 𝔊𝔯𝔢𝔢𝔫𝔢 𝔤𝔬𝔢𝔰 𝔖𝔬𝔲𝔱𝔥

before prevailed. He reached Charlotte, North Carolina, December second, and relieved Gates, who had since his defeat at Camden gathered the available militia of the state to the number of two thousand, to replace his lost army. These troops were raw and undisciplined, but with Steuben and Lee, whom Congress had assigned to the Southern department, Greene set about the work of fitting them for service, while they also formed a nucleus for gathering recruits.

In appointing Greene to the command of the Southern division, Washington had deprived his army of a strong general, but he was content in the knowledge of the special fitness of Greene for the duty to which he was assigned. His notable service as quartermaster-general after the failure of the Board of War, and his eminent ability in the field, were considerations that impelled Washington to urge his appointment to this post after the destruction of Lincoln's army at Charleston; but Congress, enamoured of Gates, chose the latter. In the interval since that time the contrast of ability in the two men had become apparent even to Congress. While Gates hurried to destruction in the South, Greene gained fresh honors in New Jersey, where he checked Clinton's advance at Springfield and sent him in retreat to Staten Island.

Incursions of this character were the extent of British activity in the North during the spring and summer of 1780. Washington had moved into New Jersey and driven out Knyphausen, whose force was greatly superior, before Clinton arrived from Charleston; and while the latter was engaged in his abortive raid, the American commander defended his position on the Hudson. His army, impoverished and reduced in numbers through the incapacity of Congress, was reinforced by the arrival at Newport, Rhode Island, July tenth, of a powerful French fleet under Admiral Ternay, bringing Count de Rochambeau with six thousand soldiers. The strength of the allied forces was thus sufficient to imperil the British at New York, and their outlying posts were finally abandoned for the better protection of the larger interests.

At the British headquarters, and in the heart of the American councils, events were making for one of the saddest burdens that Washington, in

Alexandria Va.

Arrival of French Allies

all the misfortunes of the Revolution, was called upon to bear. Benedict Arnold, whose name is now identified with treachery, was at that time one of the most valiant officers in the patriot army. Impetuous and ardent, he was ever at the forefront of action, and his self-ignoring courage inspired those about him to victorious effort in the face of impending disaster. He had led a starving army through the northern wilderness to Quebec, his energetic struggle for the control of Lake Champlain had delayed by a year the British advance to the Hudson and operated for its final defeat, and his resurgent valor at Saratoga turned the tide of battle in favor of his cause. The elements of character that contributed to these worthy ends were equally potent in self-seeking baseness, when the high impulse of patriotism had given place to one of personal gain and revenge. The wound received by Arnold in the charge at Saratoga incapacitated him, temporarily, for active service, and when sufficiently recovered he was put in command of Philadelphia, which the British had then recently evacuated. Here he married the daughter of a Tory, and formed associations that opened the way for later operations. Life at the capital developed the weaknesses of his nature, and he became involved in difficulties that brought him successively before a committee of Congress and a court-martial ; the former exonerated him, but the latter, though acquitting him of the charges preferred, qualified the verdict by directing Washington to administer a formal reprimand. The harshness of this measure was greatly miti-

Washington's Headquarters Richmond Va.

Major=General Benedict Arnold

gated by the implied praise which Washington, who admired Arnold and believed him wronged, incorporated in the rebuke; but to Arnold it was no less a rebuke, and it weighed in turning him from a life of honor to one of ignominy.

Smarting under his wrong, real or fancied, and looking to the possibilities of personal emolument, he opened cautious communication with the British, who saw in this an opportunity of acquiring by treachery what they could not take by force of arms. The American fort at West Point, on the Hudson, was coveted, and Arnold set out to obtain the post of commandant that he might work its ruin, for which he was to receive a large money consideration and a commission as brigadier-general in the British army. Though Washington had other plans for Arnold's employment, such was his regard for the man, that he deferred to the lat-

School=house of Randolphs and Jeffersons Tuckahoe Va.

ter's wishes, and the first requirement of the plot was effected. From possession it was but a step to delivery; but that step was carelessly executed by Major André, the British emissary sent to meet Arnold and arrange the details, and while on his way back to the Vulture, a sloop-of-war which had brought him up the river, he was captured at Tarrytown and the full import of his mission discovered. John Paulding, David Williams and Isaac Van Wart, the vigilant rangers who seized André, took him, in spite of liberal offers for liberty, to the American headquarters at Northcastle; and a few days later he was hanged at Tappan, after having confessed to being a spy, and notwithstanding strenuous efforts on the part of Clinton to save his officer's life. Through a blunder of the officers to whom André was delivered, Arnold was notified of the failure of his conspiracy and succeeded in escaping to the British on the day, September twenty-fifth, that the surrender was to have taken place.

To Washington, who arrived unexpectedly at West Point on the morning of Arnold's flight, the moral disappointment was particularly severe. Arnold was a valuable officer, but the gap which he left could, in a way, be filled. The real calamity was the shaken confidence in human integrity engendered by the perfidy of one so highly esteemed, and who owed so much to the kindly consideration of his superior. It opened unconsidered possibilities of defeat, and such was the improbability in Arnold's case that no limit could be set to unwelcome suspicion. Happily no further cause for such existed, and the treason of Arnold remains the one blot on the record of patriotism.

Arnold's Treachery

Westover James River Va.

In the North the year 1780 closed as it had passed, without important aggression by either side. To Washington, in his quarters in New Jersey, the outlook was cheerless in the extreme. All the old familiar besetments of failing men and scant supplies harassed him with stubborn persistence. As an executive body Congress was a failure, and Washington's strenuous entreaties were received with indifference and apathy. The lack of funds was the most serious difficulty, and after its own conspicuous failure in this field, Congress, with unusual discernment, shifted the burden to an individual of large means and earnest patriotism, by appointing Robert Morris, of Philadelphia, to be Superintendent of Finances. In the early days of the war, Morris had answered Washington's appeal with fifty thousand dollars raised on his personal credit, and, though the task was one that few men would have cared to undertake and fewer still have succeeded in, he now applied his ripe business ability to the problem, and with the coöperation of Gouverneur Morris, of New York, established a bank and raised the credit of the government on the strength of his own acceptance of the trust. The money thus available was of immense assistance to Washington, enabling him to recoup his army at a most critical time, when, as later developments proved, unreadiness would have been fatal.

Benedict Arnold, with his commission from King George, had been sent to ravage Virginia, and with Cornwallis and Tarleton in the Carolinas, the importance of the British strength in the South was clearly apparent to the American commander. He dispatched Lafayette with twelve hundred men to meet Arnold, who was burning and

Robert Morris

pillaging with the energy that had been characteristic of his worthy efforts. Early in March, Lafayette reached Annapolis, at which place he was to join the French fleet which had been sent from Newport to convoy him to Portsmouth, where Arnold was entrenched. The plan was frustrated by the appearance of a British fleet under Arbuthnot near the entrance to Chesapeake Bay, and as a result of the ensuing action the French were obliged to return to Rhode Island, leaving Lafayette without the means of reaching Arnold. Clinton, though yet with no plan beyond disconnected raids, sent General Phillips with two thousand men to join Arnold, whom the former was to relieve of command. His mission thus rendered hopeless, Lafayette was ordered to join Greene, who was beginning to make his presence felt in the farther South.

One of the typical figures of the war was Daniel Morgan of Virginia. Born to humble station, he served as private in the early Indian wars, and at the outbreak of the Revolution raised a regiment of Virginia riflemen and hurried to the front. His men formed an important part of the expedition to Quebec and were prominent in many later actions, notably at Saratoga, where they won the praise of the enemy. Morgan had not received the recognition his achievements merited and had withdrawn to his Virginia plantation, when Gates's defeat at Camden revealed the desperate situation of the cause in the South. Repressing personal considerations, he made haste to join Gates, and soon received from Congress a commission as brigadier-general. He was engaged in organizing his troops when Greene arrived, and with the approval of the latter he moved to the westward, and gathering the militia, stopped the ravages of loyalists in that section. Cornwallis watched with apprehension Morgan's growing power, and sent Tarleton, with his light infantry, to check his operations. Morgan retreated before him until he reached a favorable position at Cowpens — on the boundary between North and South Carolina — where he established himself, and instructing and encouraging his men, he waited in battle order for the British to come up. They arrived on the seventeenth of January and dashed upon the Americans with an impetuosity calculated to break the ranks of the latter; but they were prepared for this and met the assault boldly, changing formation to bring fresh troops to the front, and then by a partial retreat led the British forward, enabling a division under Colonel Washington to attack them in the rear. Met by fire before and behind, the enemy soon succumbed in unconditional surrender. Tarleton himself escaped, but upwards of six hundred of his men fell into the hands of the Ameri-

Gate Post Westover

Morgan's Victory at Cowpens

cans, with all the arms and baggage of the command. Morgan's victory was a brilliant one, his force being inferior to that of his adversary, and was largely the result of clear judgment and careful planning, backed by experienced troops.

Although Tarleton's command was destroyed, it was dangerous for Morgan to remain within reach of Cornwallis, who was sure to retaliate for the loss of his favorite regiment; and as soon as the battle was over a rapid retreat was begun, which,

Gate Westover

before the next morning, had carried the Americans well beyond the Broad River. Events proved the wisdom of this course, and the advantage thus gained barely sufficed to save them from the pursuing army, which was lightened by burning its heavy baggage, that the chase might be unimpeded. Greene also realized the importance of outwitting Cornwallis, and on learning of the victory started at once to join Morgan, at the same time sending messengers ahead to gather boats at all the rivers on the line of march, that everything might be in readiness when the troops arrived. Without this foresight all the strenuous efforts of Morgan would have come to naught, as successively at the Catawba and the Yadkin the Americans had only the river between them and their pursuers.

Greene's army, following close upon its general, joined Morgan's division at Guilford, the ninth of February, and together they continued the flight to the Dan, where Kosciuszko, sent ahead by Greene, was preparing defences. The British were so close behind that it was only by employing a rear guard to engage them in skirmishes that the Americans succeeded in crossing the river; when this was safely accomplished the skirmishing party followed rapidly, leaving the enemy baffled at the bank. The British had no boats, and as it was out of the question to ford under the fire of the Americans, they withdrew and gave up the chase.

Greene soon returned to the country south of the Dan, and for some weeks harrassed Cornwallis by raids on outlying divisions, and by intercepting his recruits and supplies. Every attempt to reach the Americans was frustrated by a rapid change of position, and after seriously fatiguing his army to no purpose, Cornwallis withdrew to rest his men and seek recruits. This gave Greene a like opportunity, and the militia, for which his aides had scoured the neighboring states while the British were being held in check, began to arrive in appreciable force. When sufficiently strengthened, Greene, who saw the necessity of a battle which should cripple his adversary, even though himself obliged to retreat, marched to Guilford Court House, which he

Morgan's Retreat

had selected as an advantageous position.   The next day, March fifteenth, the British accepted the challenge and boldly opened the attack.   Greene's forces, which number-ed somewhat over four thousand, were largely untrained militia, and at the first charge of the enemy, the firing line, thus constituted, broke and fled without offering any effective resistance.   The Continentals, who were next behind, fought with steady regularity and twice repulsed the British, who only saved the day by the reck-less use of artillery fired through their own ranks.   Greene withdrew in good order, but minus a large part of the militia, which failed to return after the first rout.

Cornwallis, who lost in the neighborhood of six hundred men, took up his march to Wilmington to refit before coming northward.   Greene immediately followed him, although defeated and with his force reduced by desertion — his loss in battle being less than a third that of the British; but he was compelled by the continued desertion of militia to abandon the pursuit at the Deep River when almost up with the enemy.

With the British forces divided, as they were by Cornwallis's expedition to Virginia, it became necessary for Greene to choose between following the former to the North, and the alternative of moving against Lord Rawdon, who held Camden and a chain of fortified posts in South Carolina.   He chose the latter plan, and quickly with-drawing from the vicinity of Cornwallis, that the latter might not detect his purpose in time to obstruct his movement, he marched for Camden, April second, and arrived that night at Hobkirk's Hill, within a short distance of the enemy's works.   Rawdon, think-ing to surprise Greene, whom he knew to be as yet without artillery, led an attack early

on the morning of April seventh, and succeeded in dislodging the Ameri-cans.   Greene was sur-prised, but not unpre-pared, as he had camped his army in battle form to guard against this possi-bility.   The struggle was sharp, and for some time the advantage appeared to be with the Ameri-cans, but at a critical moment one of those unnecessary weakenings, which had turned the scale against them on many other occasions, broke the formation, and seeing the inevitable re-sult, Greene withdrew his men while yet pos-sible to do so without sacrifice.

Reinforcements reached Rawdon a few

**Post Finials
Westover**

Greene's Campaign

weeks later, in spite of Lee and Marion, who, at the first inception of the plan, had been sent to cut off his supplies. With this added force, Rawdon started out early in May to reach, by a détour, a position in Greene's rear, which he hoped to find unguarded. The sagacious general was not to be caught in such a simple manner, however, and changed his position for one so strong that the British feared to attack. Unable to dislodge Greene, and threatened by the latter's outlying divisions, which had already taken Fort Watson, one of his important posts, Rawdon abandoned Camden, May tenth, and moved to the sea-coast. On his way he hoped to strengthen the garrison at Fort Motte, but he was too late, and arrived May twelfth, just in time to witness its surrender. Sumter had taken Orangeburg the day before, and Neilson's Ferry and Fort Granby fell within a few days. Lee and Pickens with their divisions entered Georgia and captured Fort Galphin, May twenty-first, reaching Augusta, their objective point, a few hours later. Here they met determined resistance. The two forts, Grierson and Cornwallis, were besieged, and the former, which was the weaker, was soon taken by Pickens, enabling him to go to the assistance of Lee, whose operations had so far had little effect on the strong garrison of Fort Cornwallis, which fought gallantly and held out with stubborn tenacity. The Americans were no less determined, however, and gradually weakening the defense by daily engagements, they finally assaulted the fort on June fifth, and forced its surrender.

One of the strongest British posts in the South, and after the fall of Augusta the only one in that section remaining in their control, was Ninety-Six, Georgia. To this Greene directed his attention after recuperating his army, and opened systematic

Farmington, Charlottesville Va.

Designed by
Thomas Jefferson

Sumter, Lee and Pickens

Court House, Williamsburg Va.

Designed by Sir Christopher Wren

siege operations, which, with the help of Lee, who had joined him after the victory of Augusta, had reduced the strong garrison to a point where surrender could not be long delayed, when the Americans received word of the approach of Lord Rawdon, who had again left the seaboard to come to the relief of the besieged post. Greene, who was too weak to cope with such a force, reluctantly withdrew and led Rawdon a futile chase from point to point, until the latter, unable to disperse the Americans, and fearing to remain in the position he had come so far to sustain, withdrew from Ninety-Six, taking the garrison and loyalists, and returned finally to the coast. Thus the purpose of Greene's campaign, apparently frustrated, was accomplished by the force of conditions his earlier work had created.

Detachments of the American troops followed the retreating British to the outskirts of Charleston, harassing them and preventing scattered raids and pillage. They also, as a result of engagements with outlying commands, captured upwards of one hundred and fifty prisoners, among whom were a number of officers.

Lord Rawdon embarked for England early in July, and his successor, Lieutenant-Colonel Stewart, undertook to reoccupy the country from which Rawdon had been driven. He started, late in August, with between two and three thousand men, and camped on the Santee near Fort Motte. Greene, who was encamped in the neighboring hills, had rested and strengthened his army, and he set out on receipt of information of Stewart's movements, to intercept the latter and at the same time to assail his communications by detachments in his rear. This plan was so successful that the British were obliged to withdraw to Eutaw Springs, some twenty miles down the river. Here they selected a strong

Crogan Place Locust Grove Ky.

position and awaited the Americans, who reached that vicinity September seventh, but were undiscovered until the morning of the eighth, a short time before they were ready to attack. The armies were evenly matched, and although the Americans pressed steadily forward and easily destroyed the enemy's outer lines, the resistance was able and determined, and for a while seemed sufficient to hold the ground. At this point Greene's superior tactics prevailed, and the Continentals, being formed in to replace the exhausted militia, which had so far borne bravely the brunt of the battle, charged the British before they had time to recover from the fire of the militia, and penetrating their line, drove them in disorder to the shelter of a brick building about which the camp was set. Unfortunately the victors were over-confident of success and scattered in search of plunder, with the result that the British were enabled to gather sufficient strength to render the final outcome doubtful, and Greene, bitterly disappointed, yet ever watchful of the safety of his army, felt compelled to withdraw and trust to the severity of the blow he had inflicted to force the enemy to retreat. He took with him five hundred prisoners, making the British loss, with those left on the field, nearly a thousand; which, as was anticipated, decided Stewart to return to the coast, where the protection of the British ships formed their only stronghold. As before, detachments under Marion and Lee followed and harassed the retreating army, which, to be less encumbered, destroyed large quantities of stores, and left behind more than a thousand stands of arms. Greene retired, according to his custom, to gather reinforcements, and later moved to the vicinity of Charleston, where his presence served to restrain the British and check their raids on the surrounding country; but his work was practically done, and the South, the most cruelly devastated section of the Union, was, with the exception of a few points on the coast, freed from British dominion.

Simultaneously with these victories in South Carolina came the master-stroke of the Revolution, — the operations about Yorktown which led to the surrender of Cornwallis. The successive raids into Virginia had attracted attention to that quarter,

Eutaw Springs

but the expedition under Phillips that added two thousand men to Arnold's already strong force, and Cornwallis's approach from the South, gave to the situation there an importance not hitherto possessed.

Washington, in his survey of existing conditions, realized the necessity of a decisive engagement that should successfully terminate the Revolution, which otherwise stood in grave danger of dissolution as a result of the apathy and incompetence of Congress, and the failure of the states not directly menaced, to continue the much-needed supplies of money and men. To this end he sought the coöperation of Rochambeau and his French troops, and the fleet under De Barras, recently arrived at Newport. The choice lay between New York and Yorktown, at either of which places the ships could coöperate with the land forces, an essential condition to the complete victory that Washington desired to ensure. His preference at first was for New York as offering the greater opportunity, and early in July a combined attack was made on the forts at the upper end of Manhattan. The attempt was fruitless as to its main issue, but it served to alarm Clinton, and caused him to withdraw further aid from Cornwallis; it also served as a feint and enabled Washington to make unsuspected preparations for carrying out the alternative plan, to attack the forces now combined and entrenched at Yorktown. This plan gained opportune encouragement by the receipt of assurance of coöperation from Count De Grasse, who was on his way from the West Indies with another and larger fleet.

Lafayette, whom Cornwallis unsuccessfully endeavored to isolate, had been joined by Wayne with his command, and together they had driven the British from the interior, engaging them at Williamsburg and Green Spring, and held them at bay at Yorktown. Neither Cornwallis nor Clinton had any idea that Washington would abandon New York with his main army, and this, with the operations already attempted, and the elaborate preparations made by the latter with the apparent purpose of continuing on the same lines, enabled the allied armies to slip away, leaving only a detachment to hold the British to Manhattan, and get well out of reach before Clinton discovered their absence. When he became aware of the movement he vainly endeavored to divert them from their purpose by sending Arnold, who had been unappreciatively ordered north by Cornwallis, into Connecticut to ravage and excite the country. Forts Trumbull and Griswold, near New London, were taken, and at the latter, Colonel Ledyard and nearly a hundred of his men were murdered, after having surrendered in good faith. New London was burned to complete the wanton destruction.

The armies under Washington crossed the Hudson August nineteenth, and marching through Philadelphia, arrived September eighth at the head of Chesapeake Bay, where they gathered transports and awaited the French fleet. De Grasse had

𝔉rankfort Ky.

Designed by
Thomas Jefferson

𝔐ovements of 𝔄llied 𝔉orces

Clark House
Mulberry Hill Ky.

arrived at the entrance to the Chesapeake and was landing troops sent to reinforce Rochambeau, when a British fleet under Admiral Graves appeared off the capes, and the French at once went out to meet it. The ensuing action, while not eminently decisive, was severely felt by the British, who lost one ship and were obliged to sail north to refit. On his return, De Grasse found awaiting him the squadron under De Barras, who had eluded the English fleet sent to intercept him, and arrived safely with transports and siege tools, and together they proceeded up the bay and brought down the troops, which were landed at Williamsburg, September twenty-sixth. Joined by Lafayette and the French reinforcements, the combined armies, numbering in the neighborhood of sixteen thousand men, took up positions about Yorktown, September twenty-eighth, and laid down the first lines of the siege.

With the river, against which the town was set, and Gloucester Point, opposite, in the hands of the enemy, Yorktown was ill-adapted to successful defense, and Cornwallis soon found himself surrounded with steadily approaching armies. His first position was in trenches outside the town, but he was soon obliged to withdraw to the inner fortifications, while the besiegers occupied his abandoned works. Day by day the lines contracted and the heavy guns battered the defenses with steady effectiveness. October fourteenth two outlying redoubts were taken, one by the Americans and one by the French, and Cornwallis, realizing the desperateness of his situation, resolved to stake all on an attempt to escape by the river. On the night of the sixteenth he embarked a detachment of his men which reached the opposite bank in safety, but the sudden advent of a storm frustrated his plan, and the troops already over were with difficulty brought back the following day.

His last hope gone, Cornwallis sought terms of surrender, and on the eighteenth the articles were signed. The next day eight thousand men laid down their arms to the Americans, and the British ships with a thousand more were delivered to the French. The ceremony was very imposing, the conquered army assuming all the dignity permitted by the articles of surrender. Cornwallis remained in his quarters under plea of sickness, presenting his apologies to Washington through General O'Hara, who also delivered the British commander's sword to General Lincoln, whom Washington, as a slight recompense for the former's like humiliation at Charleston, had appointed to receive it.

The careful plan had been wrought out, the overwhelming blow had been struck;

Cornwallis surrenders

Tryon Palace New-Berne N.C.

and although it could not be immediately known, the end of the Revolution had come. To Washington there yet appeared much need of continued effort, and great exertion was required on his part to prevent an easy relaxation after such a notable victory. King George was still insistent for war, and the British still held New York and Charleston.

Further reinforcements were sent to Greene, who continued to watch Stewart at the latter place, and Washington withdrew his army to the highlands of the Hudson. Clinton, with late awakening to the danger of Cornwallis's position, had started with a relief expedition and arrived at the entrance to the Chesapeake five days after the surrender. He immediately returned to New York, where the winter was quietly spent, and in the spring was succeeded by Sir Guy Carleton, whose appointment marked the accession of the peace party in Parliament, and whose mission was as much diplomatic as belligerent.

Washington's fear of further aggression and his appeals for continued vigilance, while justified by considerations of ordinary caution, and the unchanged attitude of King George, were happily unfounded, and events slowly but inevitably forwarded the termination of the war.

In England, irresistible surgings of public opinion were steadily decreasing the balance of power held by the King and his party, and by the first of March following the surrender at Yorktown they were reduced to a minority. King George, whose every measure in the history of the war had been too late for its opportunity, still clung to the hope of crushing the rebels, but he was practically alone, and before the month had passed, Lord North, his prime minister, was forced by the opposition in Parliament to dissolve his cabinet and resign the government to the Whigs. Rockingham came in at the head of the dominant party, but he was broken in health and died soon after, his place being taken by Lord Shelburne, then secretary of state.

Franklin, to whose victories of diplomacy America's standing abroad was chiefly due, had already opened negotiations with Shelburne; and with Richard Oswald, the latter's agent, had drafted at Paris the terms of peace. After much diplomatic contention, in which

North Carolina

The End of the War

St. Michael's Church

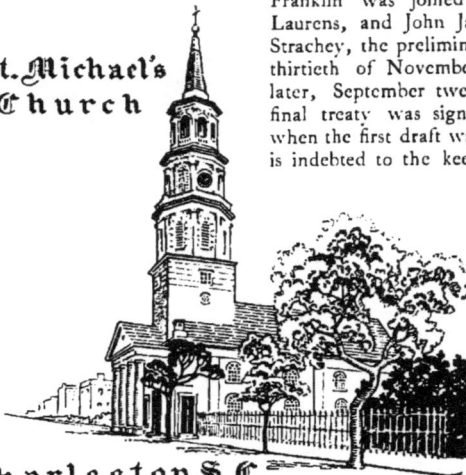

Charleston S. C.

Franklin was joined by John Adams, Henry Laurens, and John Jay; and Oswald by Henry Strachey, the preliminary articles were signed the thirtieth of November. It was nearly a year later, September twenty-third, 1783, when the final treaty was signed, but the work was done when the first draft was agreed to, and this country is indebted to the keenness and ability of its representatives, especially to Franklin, for much more advantageous terms than could reasonably have been expected.

The troubles of the embryo nation having diminished with regard to England, the looseness and insufficiency of the central government became alarmingly apparent, and the army, the only real power, from being the instrument of liberty, threatened oppression of another form. All through the war the inability of Congress to provide for the army had been an almost paralyzing difficulty, but in one way or another Washington had been able to bridge this condition and maintain an effective organization. With the war ended and the urgency of action less apparent, Congress was at the point of abandoning the soldier with no provision for arrears of pay, and no assurance of even remote recompense for the hardships endured and the battles won. The disaffection thus engendered permeated the entire army and needed but the leadership of an active spirit to rise to organized revolt. This leader was at hand in the person of Major John Armstrong, and through him the grievances of officers and men were declared in the form of a written address, in which the army was called upon to rise in its power and assume the government. Early in the previous year a somewhat similar movement had resulted in a proposition to crown Washington and declare him king ; but though touched by this evidence of devotion, his high character was proof against all allurement, and he unhesitatingly rejected the offer, denouncing the principle, and pointing out the priceless benefits of the liberty for which they had fought. This later and more determined demonstration called for more decisive action, as it was approved by the general body of officers, and a day appointed for inaugurating the plan.

Filled with grief, alike for the necessities of his men and the danger of the nation, Washington rebuked the movement in general orders, and then, calling his officers to meet him, he reviewed the seriousness of the step contemplated, and with deep emotion appealed to them to stand by him and their country, trusting to the final triumph of justice and the righting of their wrongs. Promising his continued efforts in their behalf, the general withdrew, and the officers, yielding to his entreaties,

Insurrection imminent

St. James Goose Creek S.C.

formally resolved against the uprising. Alarmed by the imminence of this peril, Congress was stirred to action, and by partial payment, and land warrants, succeeded in pacifying the troops, preparatory to disbandment.

Wayne, whom Greene had sent, soon after his arrival from Yorktown, to operate in Georgia, drove the British out of Savannah the following July, and on the fourteenth of December the same year, two weeks after the preliminary treaty was signed at Paris, they evacuated Charleston. New York was now the only port held, and Carleton occupied that uneventfully during the following year, until the signing of the final treaty, September twenty-third, was announced. He departed in state, November twenty-fifth, and as the British marched to their boats, Washington, with Governor Clinton, entered from the north and took possession. By this final act the United States were freed from British sovereignty, and the independence declared in 1776 was accomplished before the world.

His work finished, Washington called his officers about him, and bade them farewell with the simple dignity that had characterized his communion with them, but with deep emotion and fervent wishes for their future prosperity. In silence and in tears he embraced each one, and then, departing, made his way to the ferry, followed by the company, and, entering his barge, he raised his hat in final salute and began his homeward journey. What the Revolution could have been without Washington, is difficult to imagine. Through it all he stands preëminent, and continued study of his life serves but to further impress his greatness. To the wisdom and courage that planned his operations and effected them, were added nobleness and virtue that bound his army to him in bonds of love, that held when duty was forgotten.

George III, to whose unwise activity the independence of the United States is due, was, with all his deficiencies in statecraft, an honest and patriotic ruler. Surrounded by scheming and intriguing politicians, with only here and there a straightforward leader, it is little wonder that he became irretrievably committed to a policy in which there was, from his point of view, room for honest belief, and which his fawning courtiers were ever ready to extol. A complicated and disproportionate system of representation placed undue power in the hands of a few, while the great body of the people was very inadequately represented. These conditions, in times so degenerate, made it impossible for the King to gain his ends except by barter and intrigue, and we find him often the distracted victim of unfriendly and exacting cliques whose temporary strength forces recognition.

South Carolina

Charleston and New York evacuated

Believing fully in his divine right to govern, with every sentiment of hereditary prejudice outraged by the resistance of the colonists, King George, in his policy of subjection, was at least true to his natural instincts, for which we must allow while condemning the vindictive and oppressive measures resulting from it. Strong and unrelenting as was his enmity in war, his right-heartedness is evidenced by the equal sincerity of his friendliness when finally he realized the failure of his cause ; his prayer to this end expressed before Parliament, when, with emotion, he acknowledged England's defeat, that "religion, language, interest and affection might prove a bond of permanent union between the two countries," is a worthy tribute of magnanimity, but it has been tardy of fulfillment, and the century now closing has, from the beginning, witnessed strife, and jealousy, and unworthy suspicion.

Recent events, however, have clearly revealed the underlying kinship and natural sympathy of the two nations, and notwithstanding the contention which must result from the conscientious discharge of duty by representatives of these governments, a warmer friendship is assured, which it is hoped will ultimately realize the contrite benediction of King George III.

Peace

Georgia

ON THE FOLLOWING PAGES A FEW OF THE SMALLER
PIECES OF THE GEORGIAN PATTERN ARE REPRESENTED.
IT IS MADE IN STERLING SILVER ONLY (925-1000 FINE)
AND INCLUDES EVERY ARTICLE OF TABLE FLAT WARE.
A CATALOGUE FULLY ILLUSTRATING THIS LINE
MAY BE HAD FROM LEADING JEWELERS, OR WILL
BE MAILED TO ANY ADDRESS ON REQUEST.

IN adopting the Georgian Style as a motive for this design, we recognize the wide and still growing appreciation of every manifestation of colonial architecture. While this style is more nearly indigenous than any other that the changing tastes of recent years have approved, — its precedent being identified with so much that is vital in the early history of our country, and its characteristics so amenable to existing conditions, — we must remember that plans and fittings were first brought from England, where, early in the reign of George III, the reproduction of classical designs became fashionable.

Inigo Jones and Sir Christopher Wren had long before revived and adapted the teachings of Palladio and other Italian masters, and their influence prepared the way for popular acceptance of the promulgations of James Stewart, who returned, in 1762, from extended residence and study in Greece. The first fruits of the application of a style developed by the needs of public and religious life in a mild climate, to the domestic requirements of England, were absurd in the extreme; but a growing recognition of its limitations evolved the charming if not pure style with which we are familiar.

In the search for novelty its merits were for many years overlooked; but gradually the beauty of the old work has become apparent, and there is every reason to believe that the favor in which this style is now established will be lasting.

Derivation of Design

Coffee

Tea

Dessert

Tea — Reverse

Egg

Ice Cream Spoon

Chow Chow

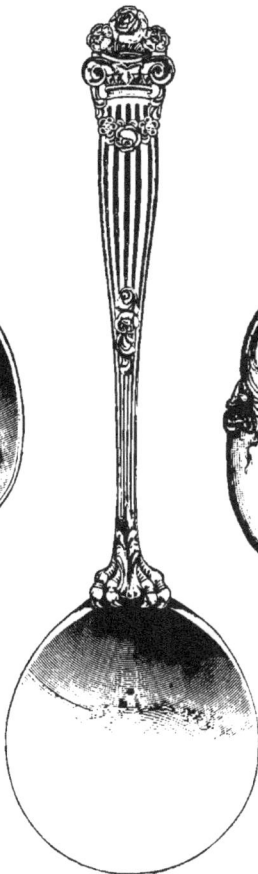

Bouillon

Salt

Chocolate

Preserve

Horse Radish

Five o'clock Tea

Jelly

Mustard

Sugar

Georgian

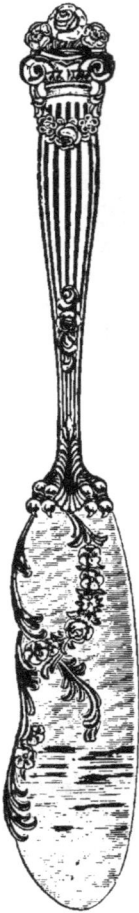

Butter Spreader

Butter Knife

Butter Pick

Hollow Handle Butter
Spreader

Lobster

Hollow Handle Dessert

Terrapin

Individual Fish

Georgian

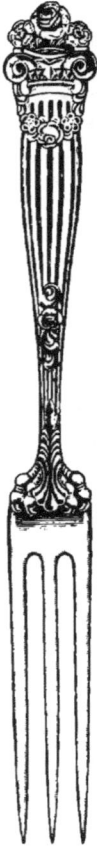

Berry

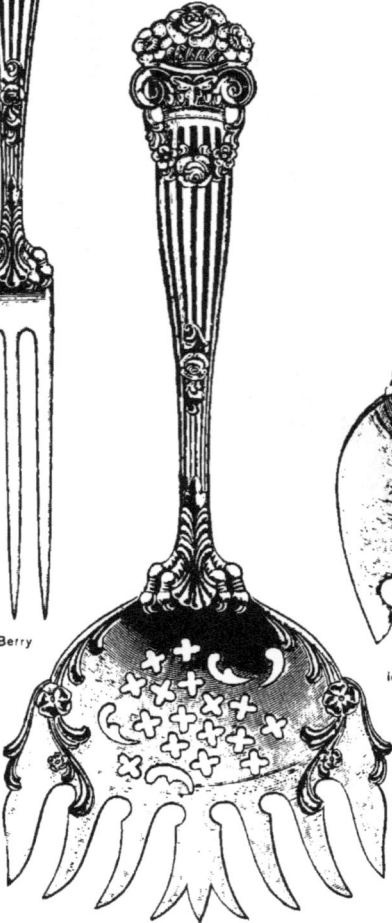

Sardine Fork

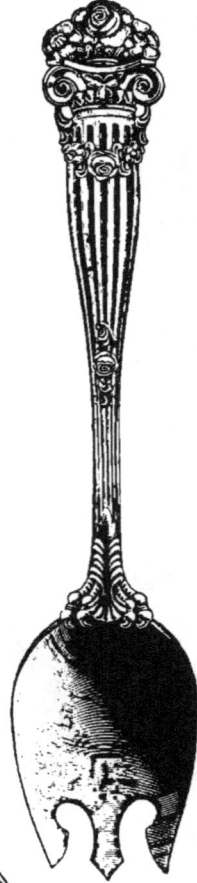

Ice Cream Fork

Pastry

Oyster

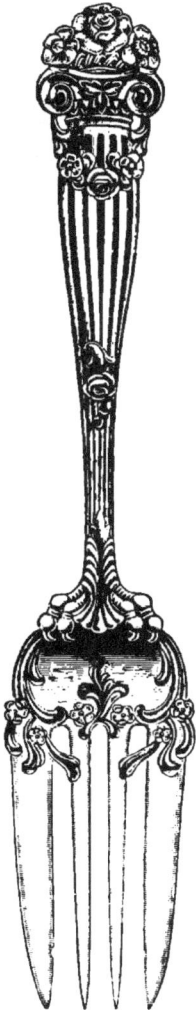

Individual Salad

Beef

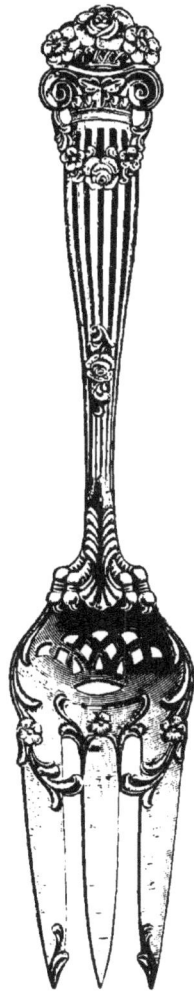

Pickle

Sardine Tongs

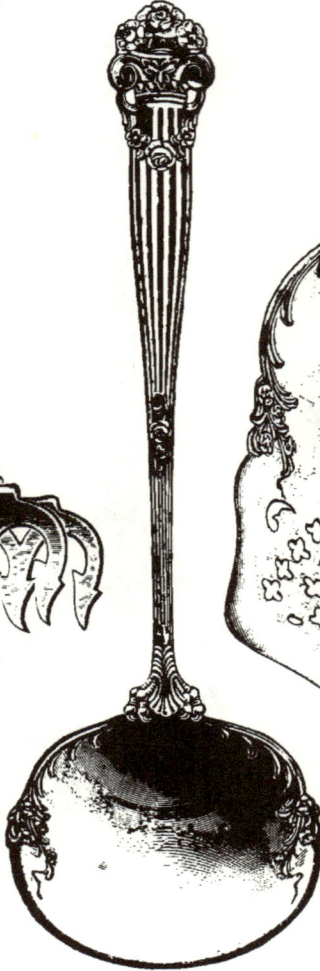

Cream Ladle

Bonbon Scoop

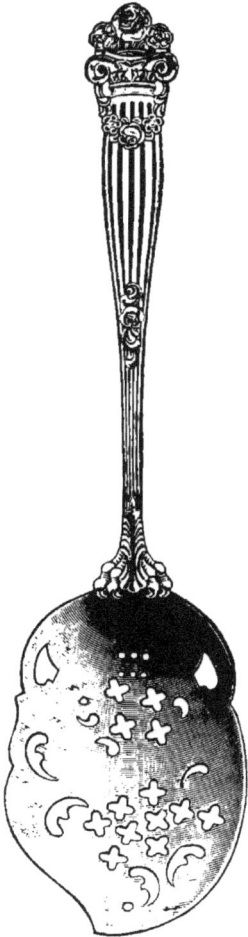

Lemon Server

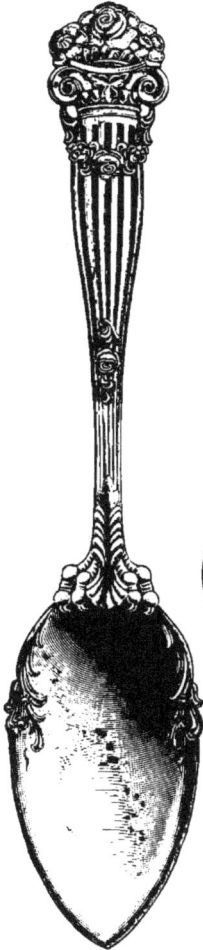

Orange

Cheese Server

Chow Chow

Sugar Shaker

Almond Scoop

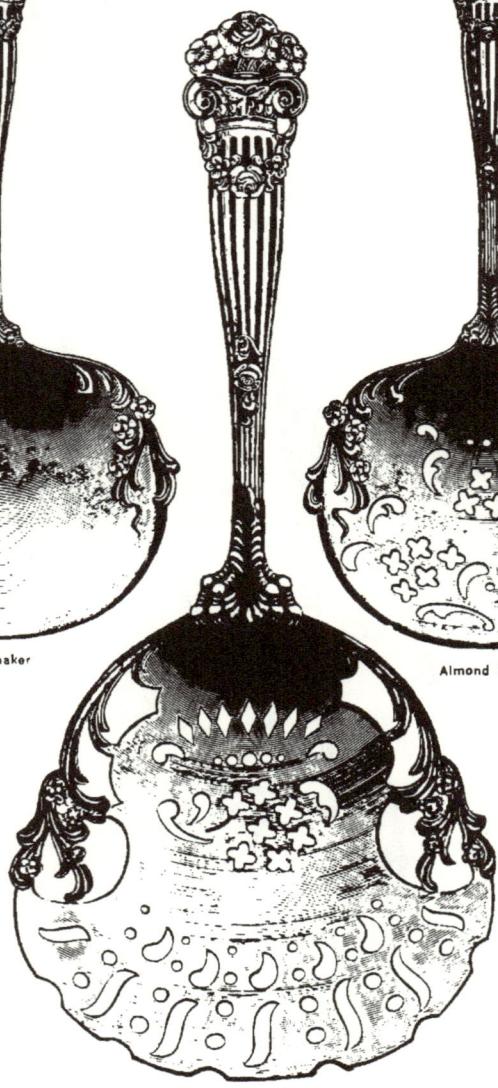

Confection Spoon

Tete-a-Tete Tongs

Sugar Sifter

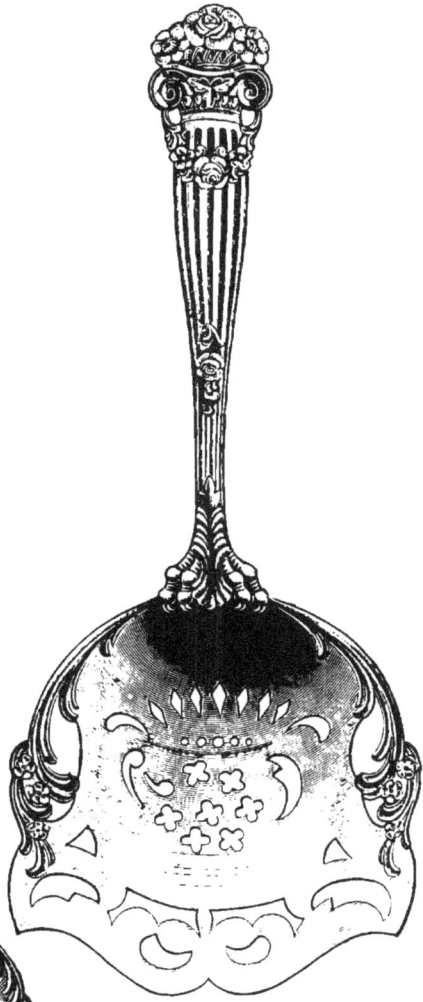

Cucumber Server

✤ ✤ A COPY OF THE
Colonial Book,
FIRST SERIES, IN
WHICH ARE PICTURED
AND DESCRIBED MANY
HISTORIC PLACES IN
NEWBURYPORT AND
NEIGHBORING CITIES,
WILL BE SENT, ON
REQUEST, BY THE
TOWLE MFG. COM-
PANY, SILVERSMITHS,
NEWBURYPORT, MASS.,
AND CHICAGO, ILL.

COMPILED AND ARRANGED BY GEORGE P. TILTON,
OF THE TOWLE MFG. COMPANY.
PRINTED BY CARL H. HEINTZEMANN, BOSTON, MASS.

NEWBURYPORT, 1697. Whittier.
UP AND DOWN THE VILLAGE STREETS
STRANGE ARE THE FORMS MY FANCY
    MEETS,
FOR THE THOUGHTS AND THINGS OF
    TO-DAY ARE HID,
AND THROUGH THE VEIL OF A CLOSED
    LID
THE ANCIENT WORTHIES I SEE AGAIN

The
Colonial
Book

of the

TOWLE MFG. CO.

Which is intended to De-
lineate and Describe some
Quaint and *Historic* Places
in NEWBURYPORT and Vicinity
and show the *Origin* and
Beauty of the COLONIAL
Pattern of Silverware.

NEWBURYPORT

T HE history of Newburyport is variously written, and, in a way, completely recorded; but this mass of material, precious as it is, only suggests the wealth of romance centering about the old town, locked up in journals and log-books, or fading away in the memories of the few relics of earlier and more picturesque times.

The ideals of to-day, here as everywhere else, are properly business and progress on the lines of modern opportunities; and this is the same spirit of enterprise which led our progenitors of seventy-five or one hundred years ago to their undertakings by sea and land, and brought them riches and renown in such generous measure.

That they are interesting and picturesque is merely incidental; their purpose was as matter-of-fact and practical as any to-day, and as well attained ; but time and changed customs lend charm to their personalities, while many of their deeds are records of bravery and greatness that would be memorable under any conditions.

Going back still further, to its first settlement in 1635, on the banks of the Parker river, called by the Indians Quascacunquen and renamed by the settlers in honor of their spiritual leader, we see a band of sturdy voyagers giving up the comforts of life in the mother country for the rugged hardships of a wilderness, and between them a long and tedious passage over a stormy sea in the small vessels and with the scant knowledge of that day. Some of them had the previous summer journeyed from Boston to Ipswich, then the outpost, where they were joined by later arrivals; and traveling by land even for so short a distance being

The Colonial Book

difficult, they loaded their goods in open boats and followed the shore to the pleasant haven which had been selected for their home. They were not needy nor driven to this step for a livelihood, as one of their first acts was stock raising on an extensive scale with cattle imported from Holland, and in the company were graduates of Oxford University. They soon established a thriving "plantation," as it was then termed, and were early incorporated and represented by deputy at the General Court held in Boston to administer the affairs of Massachusetts Bay.

If we would realize the strength of purpose which sustained these colonists, we must picture the conditions which confronted them. The severity of New England winter; their isolation and lack of material resources, for almost everything must be laboriously wrought out; their danger from wild beasts and hostile Indians; and the uncertainty of those crops which meant so much for their good or ill.

That they persevered and succeeded, Newburyport is the evidence; but the story of their trials and achievements is a reproach to the easy critic of the present, who reaps with little labor benefits for which they struggled and hoped, but of which, for the most part, they had little comprehension.

That they were devout people needs no saying, their public religious worship commencing under a spreading tree, the first Sunday after their arrival. That they also recognized the needs of the body as well as the soul, is evidenced by the license granted by the General Court to one of the settlers, within six months of their arrival, to keep an ordinary, or inn, for the entertainment of such as needed. This community was early in establishing important enterprises which, with the systematic parceling out of the land and the development and management of current affairs, gave them abundant occupation and shows their remarkable energy and business capacity. The descendants of these pioneers occupy practically the same lands to-day, which are among the most prosperous farms of the region.

The growth of the town was to the northward, and soon from the shelter of the "Oldtown" hills the settlement stretched

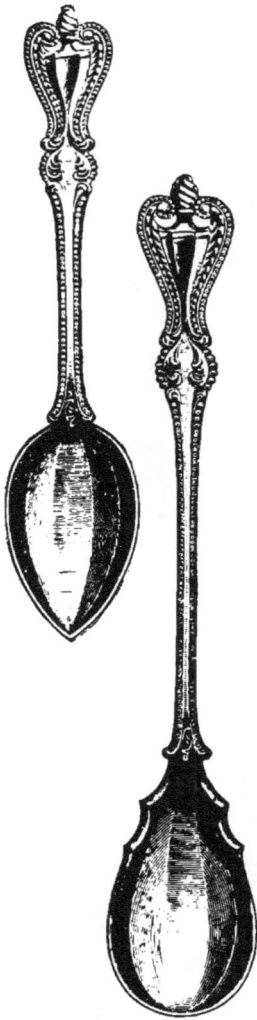

The Colonial Book

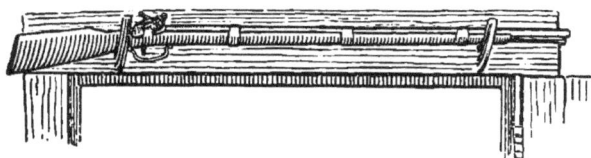

along the bank of the Merrimac, and, embracing eagerly the
opportunities it offered, encouraged maritime enterprises in every
way, until with the building of wharves and the establishment of
ship-yards began the era which was to give to Newburyport its
real power and position.   The small vessels for fishing became
numerous, and were followed by larger and more pretentious
craft, which carried to foreign ports the products of the country,
and brought back the rich goods and outfittings needed in the
rapidly developing community, or distributed through surrounding and inland towns.

Through this commerce came wealth and culture, and many
are the evidences of magnificent living among the rich merchants,
while the numerous ship-masters returned from foreign lands with
minds broadened and stimulated by contact with other peoples
and tastes formed which greatly modified the old Puritan customs.

The town furnished many troops for the Colonial and Indian
wars, and was foremost in the demonstration against the Stamp
Act, also heartily supporting the Revolutionary war from the first
Lexington alarm.   In these troops were officers of high rank
whose deeds of valor are national history.

The naval forces were greatly strengthened by ships built
here, and from here also numerous privateers sailed with letters
of marque and returned with rich prizes to be in turn fitted out

View of River Front and Shipping

on the same errands. Many are the thrilling tales of capture, imprisonment, and escape told by the returning heroes, and it is small wonder that with the prospect of booty and adventure active young men took naturally to the sea.

Commercial activity suffered a severe blow in the embargo placed on foreign trade by the government in 1807, and while it lasted shipping was at a complete standstill. A few years later, in 1811, came a second misfortune, in the form of the great fire which in one night destroyed sixteen acres of the business district, including nearly all the important public buildings and institutions. Though in a measure soon recovered from, these calamities served to seriously check advancing prosperity, and while later there were large importing interests they failed to reach their former importance, and have now, with changed methods of transportation, almost entirely disappeared. In their place have come mills and factories with their attendant needs and influences, bringing a larger if not a wealthier population, and it is by these that the city must continue to thrive.

The manufacture of silverware is one of these factors, which, having its beginning as shown by authentic record in the modest

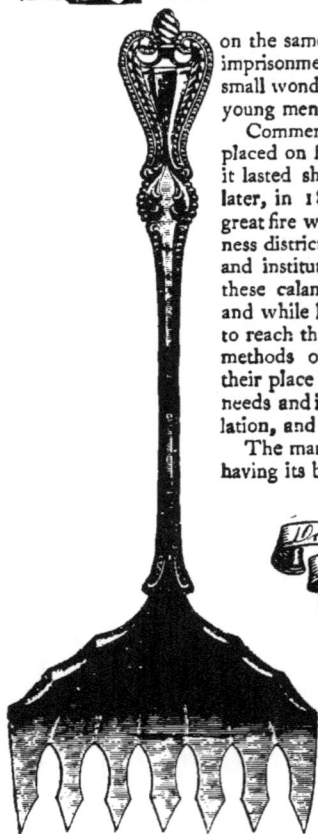

Dalton House

The Colonial Book

enterprise of William Moulton in 1689, has steadily developed until it is now one of the most important industries; and it is especially fitting that a Colonial pattern of spoons and like tableware should be produced where one of the first silversmiths of the country worked, and established a business which has been continued without interruption to the present day.

It is interesting to note in this connection that here was born Jeremiah Dummer, who, in 1659, was apprenticed to John Hull of Boston, one of the early settlers of that place and the first silversmith in America. Jeremiah Dummer, who was thus the first native American to practise this art, was afterward judge of the Court of Common Pleas of Suffolk County, and was the father of William Dummer, governor of the Province of Massachusetts.

Another Newburyport silversmith who attained prominence outside his profession was Jacob Perkins, who, in 1781, at the age of fifteen, was by the death of his master left in charge of his business, and who at twenty-one was employed to make dies for the Massachusetts Mint. He afterward became famous as an inventor, and removed to London, where his genius was recognized by the Society of Liberal Arts, and he was rewarded with their medals.

During this eventful history many men have arisen here to be enrolled among the world's acknowledged benefactors, and a few of these were noticed on another page, in connection with the places enriched by their remembrance.

The growing interest in such matters fostered by historical societies, improvement societies, and the various organizations of descendants of Revolutionary patriots, is a marked sign of the times, and to such it is hoped these pages will appeal; while to those who may visit Newburyport, they will serve as an introduction: and others, far away, may realize some of the beauties and attractions of this old New England city.

The Colonial Book

THE EARLY WARS.

IN the foregoing sketch we have briefly touched upon the part of Old Newbury, and later, Newburyport, in our country's early wars. Their record in the establishment and defence of our National government can be but outlined here, yet however incomplete this account, it seems fit at a time of such wide awaking to the glory of our past, when individuals recall with justifiable pride the services of patriotic ancestors, that the brilliant accomplishments, and also the not less glorious though unavailing efforts of a community, be indicated for the many to whom the full history is not available.

In the early expeditions against hostile Indians, Newbury took an important part, from the Pequod war two years after her settlement, in which she furnished one-fifteenth of the Massachusetts quota; the King Philip war, in which more than one-half her eligible inhabitants were enlisted; the French and Indian war, when a part of her expedition against Cape Breton was cast away and lost; to the war with the Norridgewocks, which was terminated by the killing of Sebastian Ralle, their French leader, by Lieut. Jaques of this town.

During the frequent wars between France and England, while this country was still a colony, many men went from here, to fight in England's cause on the Canadian frontier. Chief among those were Col. Moses Titcomb, Capt. William Davenport, and Nathaniel Knapp. The former, serving in many campaigns under Sir William Pepperell, took part in the capture of Louisburg and the battle of Crown Point, where he was shot while directing his regiment in most effective operations. Capt. Davenport raised companies and served in two campaigns, being with Gen. Wolfe on the plains of Abraham, and a few days later at the surrender of Quebec.

It was reserved, however, for the thrilling issues of the war of independence to call forth the universal and unwavering patriotism of the residents of old Newbury.

The story of pre-revolutionary agitation in Newburyport is one of steadily threatening protest, from the first application of

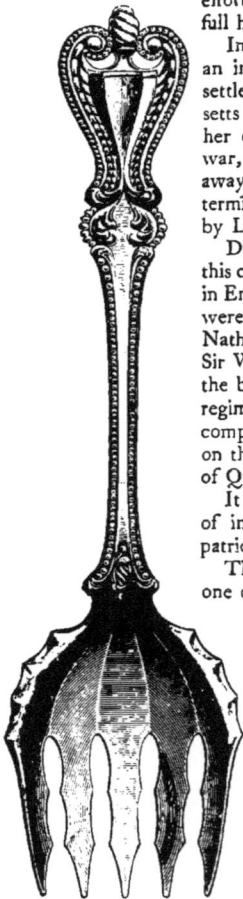

The Colonial Book

the Stamp Act. As early as 1765 a stamp distributor was hung in effigy, while visiting strangers were subjected to rough handling, if they were not quick to proclaim their antipathy to this measure. Such treatment was perforce exercised upon strangers, if at all, as in this town only four persons were suspected of loyalism and of these there was proof against but one, who died before the call to war which would have revealed his position. This was a record perhaps unequalled.

From that time to the actual outbreak of hostilities, Newburyport was in a ferment of restrained rebellion; this unity of opinion and harmony of action would have been impossible in a lesser cause, and was the more remarkable when we consider that such action meant the sacrifice of a large part of the town's greatest interest, her commerce and its dependent shipbuilding, and that the rejection of British goods meant the retirement of the many vessels in that trade.

This was the actual result; but instead of turning the people from their elected course it added to their determination, and they organized to prevent possible smuggling of the detested commodities. Under the wise and temperate leadership of the Committee of Safety, they corresponded with neighboring towns and the remoter colonies, and when the first blow was struck at Lexington it found them ready and impatient for the great struggle for civil liberty.

It was eleven o'clock at night on the nineteenth of April, 1775, when the courier bearing news of the fight at Lexington reached this town; but not a moment was lost, and before midnight the first detachment of minute-men was galloping over the road, while morning found four companies on the way to the scene of conflict. At the termination of this alarm these companies returned, but others were soon formed for regular service in the Continental army, and did memorable work at the battle of Bunker Hill.

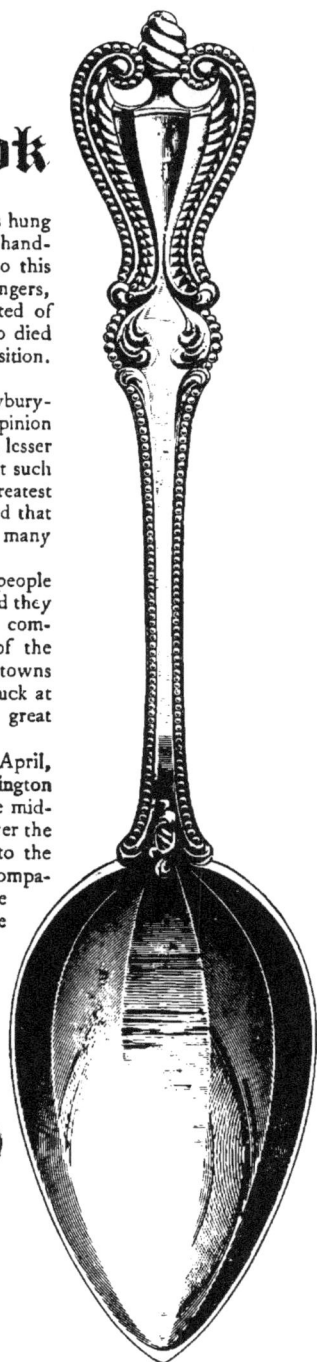

At Whittier's Birth Place. Haverhill

The Colonial Book

Space forbids following these troops through this and other battles, but a few figures rise pre-eminent, and no account, however slight, would be complete without them.

Col. Moses Little was in command of a regiment in many important battles of the Revolution, beginning with Bunker Hill, where he was officer of the day when Washington took command. On account of ill health brought on in the service, he declined the commission of brigadier general, and the command of a special expedition raised by the Commonwealth of Massachusetts.

Col. Edward Wigglesworth was appointed to a regiment early in 1776, and served with distinction for three years, when he was retired at his own request. He took a prominent part in Arnold's expedition on Lake Champlain, being third in command, and materially aided the retreat of the flotilla when it was hemmed in by the enemy.

Captain, afterward Major, Ezra Lunt was another who served at Bunker Hill, and it is asserted that his company was formed in the broad aisle of the Old South church at the close of a sermon, in response to the pastor's appeal for volunteers; and that it was the first volunteer company of the Continental army.

Here formed and embarked the important expedition under Benedict Arnold, then a valued officer in the patriot army, which, penetrating to Quebec, assisted Montgomery in his gallant assault.

As it was with maritime affairs that Newburyport was chiefly identified, it is to the sea that we must look for her most brilliant and individual victories.

Congress soon realized that our shipping was being rapidly exterminated by the armed vessels of the enemy, and issued letters of marque to assist the feeble and barely established navy in retaliating for these encroachments; ship owners here were not slow to accept these privileges, and many privateers were fitted out and manned, often by the flower of the town's youth; one

Lowell's Home Cambridge

Devil's Den

of these, the Yankee Hero, the second of that name, sailing in 1775 under Capt. James Tracy, with twenty guns and a crew of one hundred and seventy men, including fifty from Newburyport's first families, was never afterward heard from.

The spirit that animated these bold mariners may be judged from the announcement made on the occasion of prayers in church for the success of the Game Cock, the first privateer to sail out of any port, that she hoped to "scour the coast of our unnatural enemies," though she was a sloop of but twenty-four tons. She sailed from Newburyport in August, 1775, and succeeded in bringing prizes into port.

It would be difficult to estimate the number of these privateers, but that they were numerous and successful will be understood when it is stated that twenty-four ships of which Mr. Nathaniel Tracy was principal owner, with a tonnage of 6,330 and carrying 2,800 men, captured from the enemy one hundred and twenty vessels amounting to 23,360 tons, and which with their cargoes were sold for three million nine hundred and fifty thousand specie dollars. Mr. Tracy was also principal owner in one hundred and ten other vessels, twenty-three of which were letters of marque. These vessels were closely allied to the regular navy, which was now gaining strength, and we find the same men alternating between the command of privateers and government vessels, as the fortunes of war permitted.

The frigates Boston, Hancock, and Protection, and the brig Pickering, were built here, as well as the sloop of war Merrimac which was built by subscription and tendered to the government, when its funds were reduced, to be paid for at a very low price

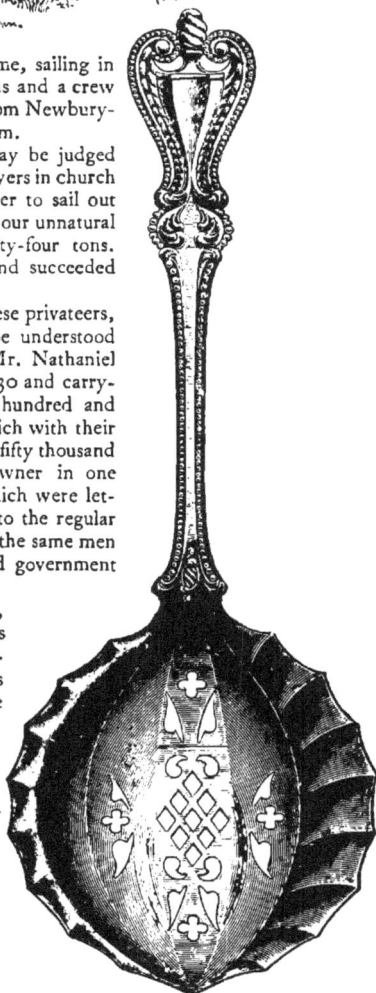

Plum Island

Col. Barrett House Concord

when convenient. She was commanded by Capt. Moses Brown of this port, a remarkably gallant sailor, and during the five years that she was in commission made many important captures.

The war ships Alliance and Warren were also built on the Merrimac, just above Newburyport, and were fitted out at this place.

The name of Paul Jones, the intrepid and irresistible "Citizen of the World," as he later styled himself, whose brilliant prowess was developed in the service of the United States, is connected with Newburyport through two of his ablest lieutenants, Henry and Cutting Lunt.

The messieurs Lunt, cousins, first shipped in the brig Dalton, Captain Eleazer Johnston, which sailed, with a crew of one hundred and twenty men, November 15, 1776. The Dalton was captured, the twenty-fourth of the following December, by the sixty-four-gun man-of-war Reasonable, of the English navy, and her crew cast into Mill Prison, Plymouth, where they remained, and suffered great hardships, for more than two years, and were finally released through the efforts of Benjamin Franklin. During this time Charles Herbert of Newburyport, one of the number, wrote a journal which he preserved in spite of the close inspection to which they were subjected. After his death this journal was published, and forms a most interesting and valuable record of life in an English prison.

Henry and Cutting Lunt, on obtaining their liberty, went to France and enlisted as midshipmen with Paul Jones, on the *Bon Homme Richard* then fitting out at L'Orient. They were speedily promoted lieutenants, and served their able commander, whom they greatly admired, in many of his fiercest engagements, in-

The Colonial Book

cluding that with the Serapis. It was in this terrible battle, when Commodore Jones was fighting against heavy odd., that his success was almost reversed by the traitorous act of his subordinate, the Frenchman Landais. The latter was in command of the ship *Alliance* before mentioned, and, inspired by jealousy, continued under the presumable excuse of firing at the enemy, to rake the decks of the *Bon Homme Richard*, in spite of the frantic signals of the latter. Many Newburyport men were in the crew of the *Alliance* at that time, and were thus obliged to fire on their friends and townsmen.

When Paul Jones was recruiting for a frigate building for him at Portsmouth, he came to Newburyport to engage Henry Lunt, and expressed great regret when he found that Lieutenant Lunt had sailed on the letter of marque ship *Intrepid*, of this port. He remarked that he would prefer Mr. Lunt to any officer he had ever known.

Many seamen from Newburyport also served under Jones in the *Ranger*, *Bon Homme Richard*, *Alliance*, and *Ariel*.

While men-of-war and privateers carried brave men to seek the enemy abroad, those left at home were far from idle. Shipbuilding was very active, forts were established and maintained at the mouth of the river, while the English ship *Friends*, which had mistaken this port for Boston, was captured off the bar, by the stratagem of adventurous spirits who had observed her actions from the town and boarded her in open boats.

In 1779 the ship *Vengeance* and the schooner *Shark* fitted out here and joined the ill-fated expedition by which it was intended to overthrow the British military post on the Penobscot, but which, after entering the harbor, was hemmed in by a large fleet

The Colonial Book

of the enemies' ships, that appeared unexpectedly. Rather than see them fall into the hands of the British, the commander of the expedition ordered his ships burned, and the crews found their way home overland.

The war of 1812 found Newburyport just recovering from the great fire of 1811, and the paralyzing Embargo of previous years. In striking contrast to their war spirit in the Revolution, the people of this town were almost unanimously opposed to this second war with England, and this not for reasons of mere commercial policy, however much they needed business, but on the ground that such a war was unjustified, and that the differences might easily be settled in other ways. An address adopted in full town meeting was sent to the legislature of Massachusetts, in which they declared their willingness to stand by the Constitution and defend their rights, and their equal unwillingness to take any aggressive part in the proposed war. These sentiments were in the main adhered to, throughout hostilities, and in pursuance of them, forts were manned at the mouth of the Merrimac and at other points on Plum Island, which served to keep at bay several English ships that hovered around this part of the coast, in the hope of destroying the sloop of war Wasp and gunboats Number Eighty-one and Number Eighty-three, then building here.

Although privateering shared to a great degree the unpopularity of the war, quite a number were fitted out here, some of which made brilliant records. Chief among these was the brig Decatur, Captain William Nichols, which, during two weeks of one voyage, captured eight vessels, four of which were armed. Earlier in the war Captain Nichols was in command of the merchant ship Alert, which was taken by the British man-of-war Semramis, and ordered to Plymouth under a guard from the latter. Before reaching that port, however, Captain Nichols

Oldtown Hill and Parker River Bridge

and his men regained control of the ship and imprisoned the British seamen in the hold. Unfortunately, they soon fell in with another British ship, the Vestal, which again took them and carried them to Portsmouth, England. This may have determined Captain Nichols to his latter course which was of undoubted service to the National cause.

Privateering, though apparently very remunerative during the war of the Revolution, did not prove so in the end, except as it stimulated business for the time being, and the enormous fortunes gained by individuals were much reduced by later losses and contributions to the expense of war. In addition to the many merchant ships captured by the English, twenty-two vessels, carrying over one thousand men, sailed from here and were never afterward heard from.

In the eight years from the battle of Lexington to the proclamation of peace, Newburyport raised for current expenses $2,522,500, which was eighty-five times the aggregate of appropriations for an equal period immediately preceding.

It was at first intended to print here the names of all who served in the Revolutionary wars, from Newbury and Newburyport, but the impossibility of this becomes apparent when we find that in the neighborhood of fifteen hundred were in the army alone, at one time or another; while the number of those that were in the navy or privateers would be difficult even to estimate. In place of this, the publishers of this book will freely send to any of Newbury or Newburyport ancestry, all available record of any name submitted, or will, in any other way possible, identify early patriots.

The Colonial Book

ALTHOUGH commerce and ship-building were the chief industrial interests of Newburyport in its early years, invention and manufacturing were by no means absent. Reference has been made to the antiquity of silversmithing here, and much more might be said of the extent of this industry, and the variety of articles manufactured. Some of them, as for instance silver shoe-buckles, are now obsolete, while silver thimbles and necklaces of gold beads, though still used, are not commonly the product of silversmiths. In 1824, machinery was invented here for the manufacture of silver thimbles, and an extensive business was developed in this line, but it has long since ceased to exist.

Many instances might be cited of great men who were trained as gold or silversmiths, but whose talents afterwards enriched other branches of art or science. In the old world, Cellini and Michael Angelo were prominent examples, and, later, Paul Revere arose in this country and rendered important services for the welfare, comfort, and prosperity of a struggling people. In like manner, Jacob Perkins, the Newburyport silversmith, whose great skill as engraver and die-cutter, as well as silversmith, is elsewhere referred to, was too richly endowed with ideas and ambition to limit his efforts to a narrow field.

He was born July 9, 1766, and died July 13, 1849, after a life of versatile activity in the mechanic arts and sciences, where, in the face of triumphs that would have satisfied many, we find him turning from one problem to another, and gaining new laurels from each. One of his most important inventions was a machine for making nails, produced when he was but twenty-four years of age. At that time all nails were forged by hand, and a good workman could produce one thousand in a day. With his perfected machines, the daily product of one man was increased to ten kegs, of one hundred pounds each.

He associated with himself Messrs Guppy & Armstrong of Newburyport, who built the machines, and together they estab-

Artichoke River Bridge

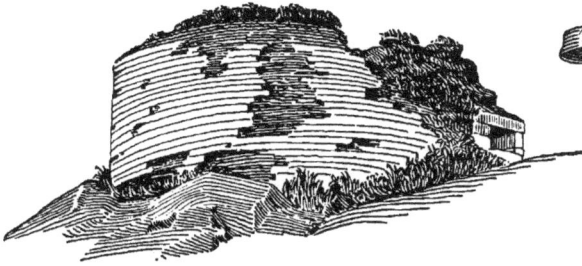

lished a manufactory at Newbury Falls, a part of the town now called Byfield, where water-power was available.

In the following extract from an advertisement in the Impartial Herald, Newburyport, 1795, we catch a glimpse of business methods in those days of quaint customs:—

The patentee would inform the public that they have begun the manufacture of brads, and will have a considerable number in fourteen or twenty days. As some will naturally think they cannot supply the whole continent and will therefore order from abroad, they would say that they have three engines which will make thirty-six hundred thousand weekly, and will add one engine each month.

N. B. A few whitesmiths may have constant employ and liberal wages.

Proprietors { Jacob Perkins, Inventor.
{ Guppy & Armstrong.

To follow in detail all the enterprises and achievements of Jacob Perkins would unduly extend this article, and we can only briefly refer to the most important.

He invented a stereotype check-plate for the reverse of bank-bills, designed for the prevention of counterfeiting. This was very successful, there being no record of an attempt to counterfeit it, whereas the practice had been very common with those previously used.

During the war of 1812, he was employed by the National government in the construction of machinery for boring out old and honey-combed cannon, and he invented a steam gun that discharged one thousand balls a minute.

He made great improvements in hardening and softening steel and particularly applied these to the engraving of that metal.

He demonstrated the compressibility of water, inventing the Piezometer for this purpose, and invented instruments for measuring the depth of the sea. On his arrival in London in 1820, he published a treatise on these subjects. He also experimented on new types of the steam engine, in some employ-

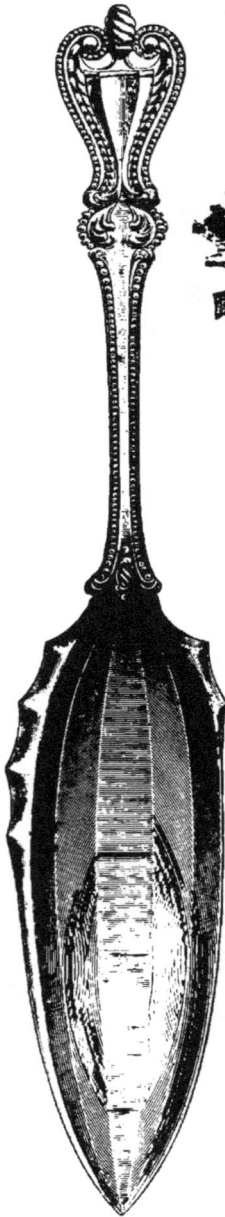

ing steam at a pressure of 65 atmospheres, or 975 pounds to the square inch.

To him all phenomena and conditions seem to have been a challenge, and he applied his powers to the solution of any problem presented. In London he was known as the "American Inventor," and was accorded much distinction.

Another industry inaugurated by Newburyport capital was located at the falls in Byfield. This was the Newburyport Woolen Company, established in 1794, the first company incorporated for that business in the state, and by some authorities named as the first woolen manufactory in America. The carding and other machines for its equipment were built by Standring, Guppy, & Armstrong, in Newburyport, being set up in "Lord" Timothy Dexter's stable; and were the first made in this country.

At Newbury a fulling mill had been in operation since 1687, when it was established by Peter Cheney, who sold it to John Pearson, by whose descendants it was operated as a fulling mill and blanket factory until destroyed by fire. It was succeeded by the present mill, established by the Pearsons, who are most prominently identified with this industry.

At Byfield, also, machinery for making wooden shoe-pegs was invented by Paul Pillsbury. This article completely revolutionized the manufacture.

Other industries that at the beginning of this century contributed largely to Newburyport's prosperity, were:—cordage-making, employing fifty hands; boot and shoe making (Newbury and Newburyport together), employing upwards of one hundred and fifty hands, these being scattered in the little shops that dotted the country in that day; comb-making, the product of which was nearly $200,000, annually; tobacco-manufacture, in the form of

The Colonial Book

snuffs and cigars; tanning; morocco-dressing; wool-pulling; carriage-building; and not least of all, distilling. Rum was a very important commodity, freely drunk by high and low; and few advertisements of merchandise were seen without the announcement of a choice hogshead of rum, generally in large type at the head of the list.

At the close of the last century there were ten distilleries in active operation here, contributing to the reputation of New England rum.

Another notable feature was Newburyport's importance as a publishing centre, and the extent of its retail book-trade.

The first newspaper here was established in 1773, by Isaiah Thomas and Henry W. Tinges, who, on December 4 of that year, issued the first number of the Essex Journal and New Hampshire Packet.

Only a few of the books published here can be alluded to, but some of these were of much importance.

The first system of Arithmetic published in this country was the work of Nicholas Pike, a Newburyport school-master, and was published here in 1787. This was a very comprehensive work, and was an authority for many years.

Blunt's famous "Coast Pilot" and other nautical works were published here by Blunt & March, who also issued many other volumes, including medical works, Bibles, Testaments, hymn books, and other religious works, such as "Christ's Famous Titles and Believer's Golden Chain, together with Cabinet of Jewels."

Other works were: Quarles' "Emblems and Hieroglyphics of the Life of Man," 1799, with copperplate engravings; "The Life of Nelson;" "The Life of Paul Jones;" "The Poetical Works of Peter Pindar, a Distant Relation of the Poet of

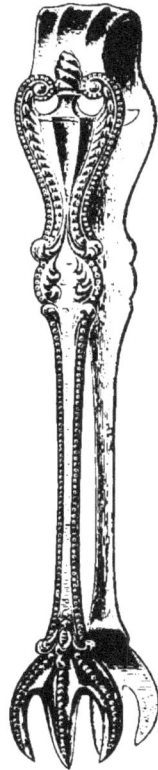

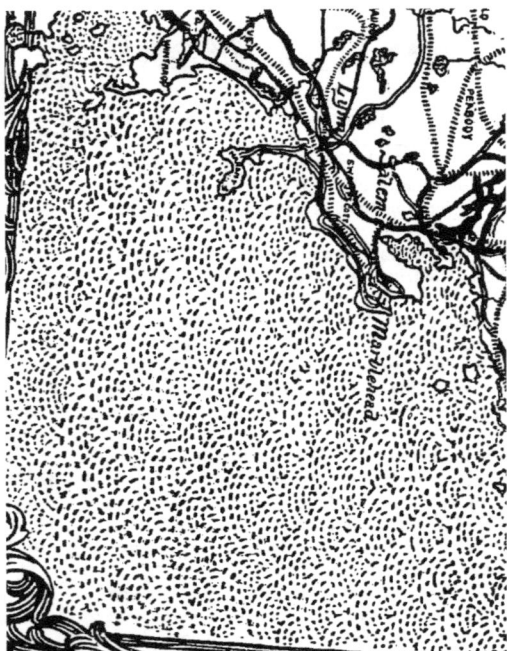

Location of Towns Mentioned.

ELECTRIC ST. RAILWAYS—EXISTING
ELECTRIC ST. RAILWAYS—PROJECTED ----
STEAM RAILWAYS
HIGHWAYS BEST FOR BICYCLING

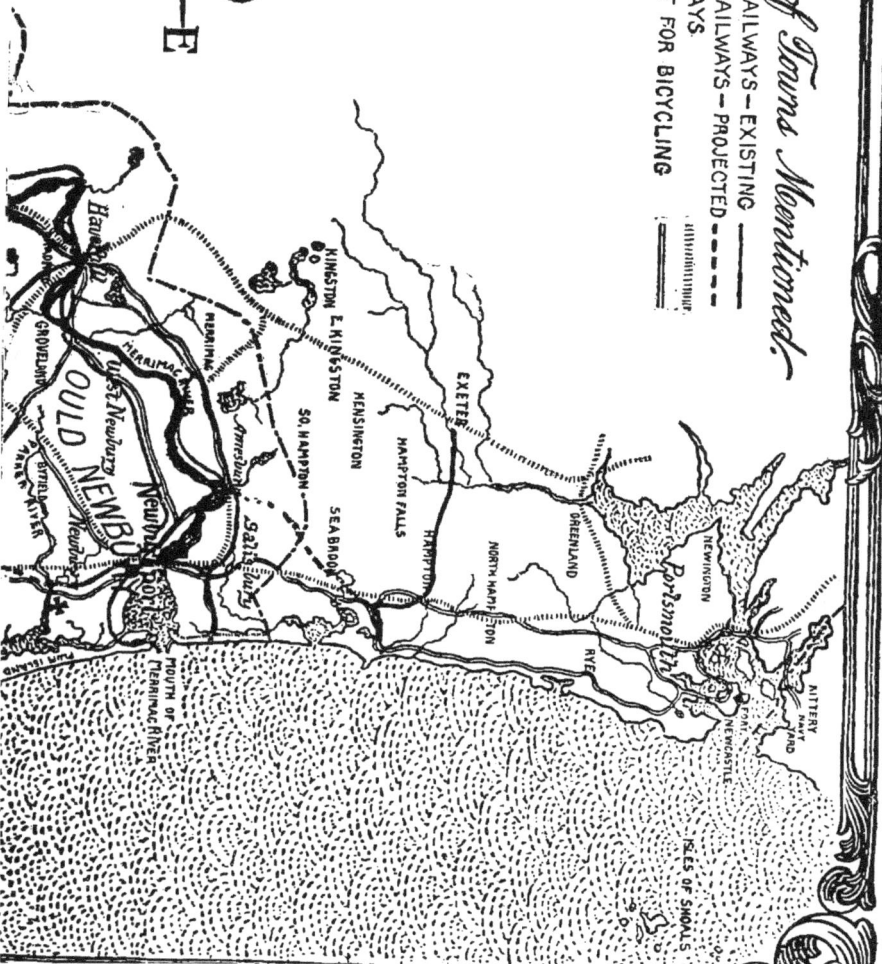

Munroe Tavern
Lexington

Thebes;" the "Idler," in two volumes; and Volume II of
"Letters Written by the late Right Honorable Philip Dorman
Stanhope, Earl of Chesterfield," Volume I of which was pub-
lished at Boston.

The publishers of these were Angier March, successor to
Blunt & March, Thomas & Whipple, and John Mycall.

An evidence of the magnitude of this business is the extensive
advertising of books in the local papers of that time, and the fact
that one of the stores burned in the great fire of 1811, contained a stock of $30,000 worth of books.

Newburyport is, or has been, more or less identified with some
of the most prominent educational institutions of the present, first
among which is Harvard College. The town of Newbury contributed to the support of this institution in its earliest years, and
had the honor of claiming its first graduate, Benjamin Woodbridge
of this town being placed at the head of the class of nine who
completed the course in 1642.

Position in the class was determined by the standing or rank
of the families of members, a method in keeping with the rigid
social distinctions of those days.

Newburyport furnished seven professors to Harvard College,
including Samuel Webber who was made president in 1806,
and Cornelius Conway Felton, who was similarly honored in
1860. Other college presidents born here were Samuel C.
Bartlett of Dartmouth, Leonard Woods of Bowdoin, and Benjamin Hale of Hobart.

Dummer Academy, Newbury, was founded by Governor
Dummer in 1761, and was the first institution of its kind in
operation in America. It has had a notable history, and is still
in a flourishing condition.

The Colonial Book

EMINENT MEN OF EARLY TIMES RESIDENT HERE, NOT ELSEWHERE MENTIONED.

Chief Justice Samuel Sewall, the subject of Whittier's poem of which the quotation on the first page of this book is the beginning, was born in 1652, and was one of the most learned and respected men of his time. He married Hannah Hull, daughter of John Hull, master of the Massachusetts Mint, referred to on another page as the first silversmith in Boston, who presented the bride with a dowry equal to her weight, in silver sixpences.

Theophilus Bradbury, a jurist of distinction and member of Congress under Washington's administration, was born here in 1739. He was also justice of the Supreme Court of Massachusetts.

Charles Jackson, a son of Jonathan Jackson, was born in 1775, and became an eminent lawyer and justice of the Supreme Court of Massachusetts.

Patrick Tracy Jackson, born in Newburyport in 1780. Merchant and originator, with his brother-in-law, Francis C. Lowell, of cotton-cloth manufacture in America. They invented machinery, and established a mill at Waltham which was in successful operation many years, and was said to be the first manufactory in the world to combine cotton spinning and weaving, under one roof. Later, Mr. Jackson purchased the entire site and water privilege of the present city of Lowell, which he founded, and named in honor of his brother-in-law and former partner, then dead. In 1830, Mr. Jackson, in company with Mr. Boot, conceived the project of constructing a railroad in New England, and, overcoming great obstacles, completed it in 1835. This was the Boston & Lowell Railroad, now a part of the Boston & Maine system.

Charles Toppan, the first president of the American Bank Note Company, was born in 1796, and studied engraving in Philadelphia. He was later associated with Jacob Perkins, with whom he went to England to introduce improvements in bank-note engraving. In 1858, he organized the American Bank Note Company of New York, with branches in Boston, Philadelphia, Cincinnati, New Orleans, and Montreal.

Jacob Little, son of a prosperous merchant of Newburyport, was born in 1797, and at an early age entered the employ of

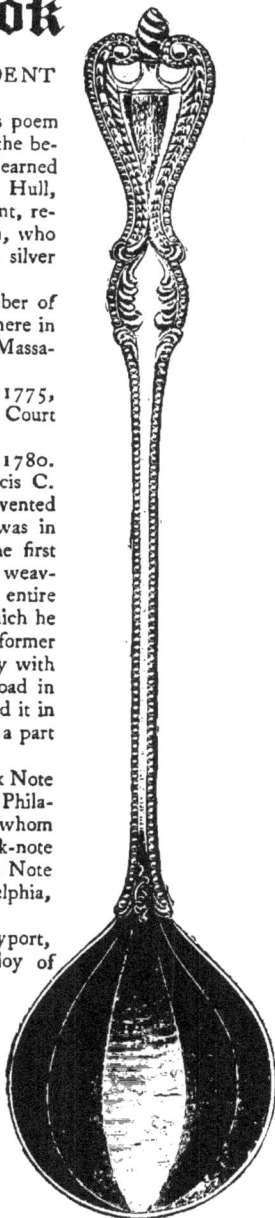

Whittier's Birth Place Haverhill

a prominent merchant of New York. He afterward became a member of the New York Stock Exchange, and was the acknowledged head of the financial world of that city.

William Wheelwright, one of Newburyport's greatest benefactors, was born in 1798. He was a ship-master, and was cast away on the coast of Brazil in 1823; which led him to settle and engage in business in South America, in the development of which he became a prominent factor. He established steamship lines and built the first railroads on that continent, overcoming tremendous natural obstacles, and finally accumulating great wealth. His statue in bronze stands in the public square of Valparaiso, the gift of the people, in recognition of his achievements.

He always retained his attachment for and interest in his native town, and in his will provided for the establishment of a scientific school here, when the fund, which now amounts to $400,000, should be sufficient. A part of the income of this sum is now used to defray the expenses of a scientific education for such graduates of the High School as desire it, some being maintained in Europe for this purpose.

Caleb Cushing, the eminent lawyer and statesman, was born in Salisbury in the year 1800, but came to Newburyport with his parents at the age of two years. He was educated for the bar, and early achieved distinction in his profession. He was minister to China and to Spain, and represented this country at the Geneva tribunal.

He was also commissioned brigadier general in the Mexican War, and held many other important offices.

Others whom Newburyport has been proud to call her sons by birth or adoption are:—

Right Reverend Thomas M. Clarke, Bishop of Rhode Island, born here in 1812.

The Colonial Book

Benjamin Perley Poore, journalist and author, born at Indian Hill Farm, Newbury, the home of his ancestors for many generations, in 1820.

General A. W. Greely, of the United States Army, commander of the Arctic Expedition bearing his name. He was born in 1844.

Mr. William C. Todd, founder of the Free Reading Room of this city, and lately donor of $50,000 to maintain a free newspaper reading room in the Boston Public Library. Mr. Todd was born in Atkinson, N. H., in 1823; and was for many years principal of the Female High School of this city.

Josiah Little, founder of the Public Library.

Michael Simpson, by whose liberality the Public Library building was greatly enlarged and improved.

George Peabody, the famous London banker, whose benefactions amounted to millions of dollars. Mr. Peabody received his early business training here in the employ of his brother, but was obliged to leave Newburyport after the great fire of 1811. He endowed the Newburyport Public Library with a fund of $15,000.

NOTES.

The quaint old sign of the Wolfe Tavern, pictured at the end of this book, is a pleasing reminder of the ancient institution of that hostelry, as well as a token of early patriotism and tribute to military greatness.

Captain William Davenport brought back from the plains of Abraham enthusiastic appreciation of his late commander, General Wolfe, who fell a sacrifice to bravery in the hour of his hard-earned victory. When, therefore, in 1762, Captain Davenport transformed his dwelling near the lower end of Fish (now State) Street to a tavern, he dedicated it to his lamented leader, and placed in front a swinging sign, elaborately carved, with a portrait of General Wolfe, surrounded by a wreath entwined with scrolls, the whole appropriately painted and gilded. This highly

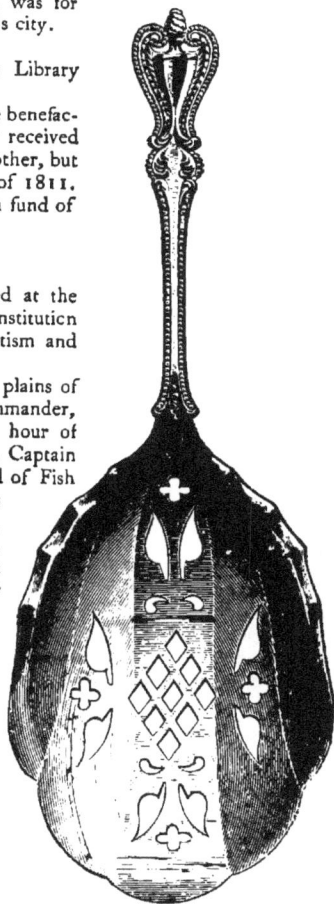

decorative emblem was freely threatened with destruction, during the Revolutionary War, when only the hatred of all things British was thought of, and former pride in the achievements of Wolfe forgotten. While all other reminders of royalty were destroyed, and notwithstanding the declaration of a local newspaper, that it was an "insult to the inhabitants of this truly republican town," it remained in place until destroyed by the great fire of 1811. The present sign was erected in 1814, when the tavern was removed to its present location.

Before the introduction of railroads, the Wolfe Tavern was the property, and a station, of the Eastern Stage Company, which ran daily trips, with relays of horses, to Boston and Portsmouth; and the arrival and departure of the stages, which, it may be noted, were all built in Newburyport, were events of considerable importance, and attended with consequent excitement. The Eastern Stage Company was the forerunner of the Eastern Railroad Company, which road is now operated by the Boston & Maine Railroad Company.

The brick building on the corner of State and Harris Streets, which was the nucleus of the present hotel building, was first occupied as a residence by Colonel John Peabody, uncle of George Peabody, and then a merchant in this town.

Two Newburyport men, members of Captain Richard Titcomb's company, were of the number that conveyed Benedict Arnold to the British ship Vulture, in September, 1780, and scorned his offer of promotion, if they would follow him in his then announced desertion from the American to the English forces.

One of the ancient institutions of Newburyport is the office of town-crier. It is now neither appointive nor elective, the present incumbent having, years ago, succeeded to it, and con-

White-Ellry House
Gloucester

Jackson House Portsmouth

tinued without opposition.   In early times he commanded attention with a drum, and one of his duties was to escort petty
culprits through the principal streets, calling attention to their
offences, which they also were sometimes required to proclaim.
The business of the present picturesque exemplar is, however,
mostly confined to announcements of excursions or entertain-
ments, varied with the promotion of retail trade, and his, "Hear
what I have to say!" is preceded by the clang of a large hand-
bell.   It is doubtful if this functionary survives anywhere else in
the United States.

The Curfew Bell, which has recently given its name to a
movement to compel the retiring of young people from the streets
at nine o'clock in the evening, has, with the exception of a short
interval in the last decade, been rung here nightly for one
hundred and ninety-two years, and it is indeed a curfew, or
signal for retiring, for many people.

The first vessel to display the American flag on the river
Thames, was the Count de Grasse, Captain Nicholas Johnson,
of this port.

A Newburyport ship, the Indus, was also the first to sail from
this country to Calcutta, after the war of 1812, and made the
return trip before news of her arrival had otherwise reached
here.

A few months later in the same year, another vessel, the
Dryad, sailed from here to carry to Calcutta the first five
missionaries of the American Board of Foreign Missions, an
organization established here by a Newburyport and a Salem
clergyman, but which has long since outgrown its early home
and removed to broader fields.

The history of ship-building at this port, includes many items
of general interest.   While it is impossible, through imperfect

registration, to ascertain the exact number of vessels built on the Merrimac, it is probable that, from first to last, the number would be upwards of two thousand.

The water-line model which enabled a designer to more easily and accurately ascertain the lines and sections of his creation, was invented here by a prominent ship-builder, Orlando Merrill, in 1794. The original model of this invention is now preserved in the rooms of the New York Historical Society.

In 1853 the celebrated clipper ship Dreadnaught was built here, a vessel whose remarkable records of crossing the Atlantic in a little more than thirteen days, were nearly equal to those of the first steamships.

Newburyport closed the record of ship-building in Massachusetts, with the launching, in 1882, of the Mary L. Cushing, the last vessel of that class built in this state.

Although the various societies of Daughters of the Revolution are of comparatively recent formation, the spirit which they represent was manifest in Newburyport as early as 1796, as shown from the following from the Impartial Herald of that year.

Newburyport, February 26, 1796. Female patriotism. A number of ladies belonging to this town met on Monday, in honor of the day that gave birth to the man "who unites all hearts," and dedicated a few glasses to the following truly sentimental and highly republican toasts.

1. May our beloved *President* preside at the helm of government longer than we shall have time to tell his years.
2. Mrs. Washington, respected consort of our illustrious chief.
3. May the fair patriots of America never fail to assert their independence, which nature equally dispenses.
4. Maria Charlotte Corday. May each Columbian daughter, like her, be ready to sacrifice their life to liberty.
5. The day that saw the wondrous hero rise shall, more than all our sacred days, be blessed.

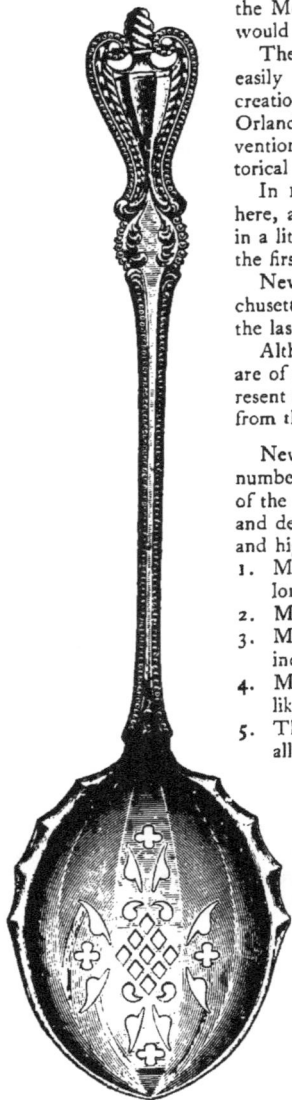

Doak House
Doak Lane
Marblehead

W HILE the purpose of this book is to give, in connection
with Colonial silverware, an outline of the Colonial and
Revolutionary history of Newburyport, it is also designed
to note briefly some of the chief points of interest in neighboring
cities and towns. This reference to its main object is made
that any seeming lack of proportion between the representation
of a place and its known importance may be understood, and the
random character of the selections accounted for.

Salem is particularly rich in points of interest around which
history or tradition has left its charm of romance or pall of tragedy.
It was here that occurred the first armed resistance of the
Revolution, when, on the 26th of February, 1775, the march
of three hundred British troops sent by General Gage to seize
munitions of war was arrested. From here came Colonel Timothy Pickering, one of Washington's most trusted advisers, and
to whom was given successively every office in his cabinet, when
the latter became president.

In addition to its wealth of history and the memories of its
once famous commerce, its heroes of war and statecraft, and its
merchant princes, Salem is remembered and particularly visited
as the home of Hawthorne and the scene of several of his romances.
His birthplace, the home of his youth, the "House of Seven
Gables," the "Grimshaw House," and Custom House, as well

First Church
in Salem
1634

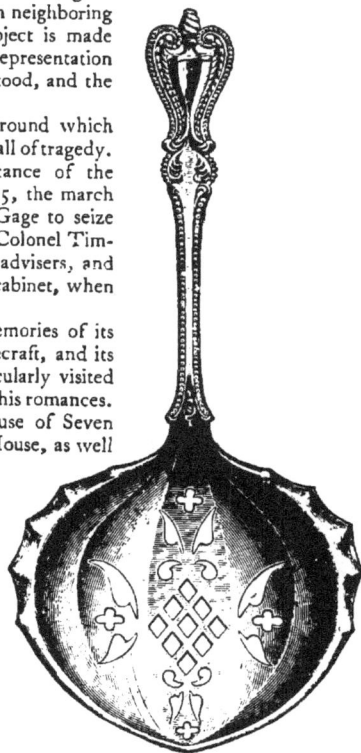

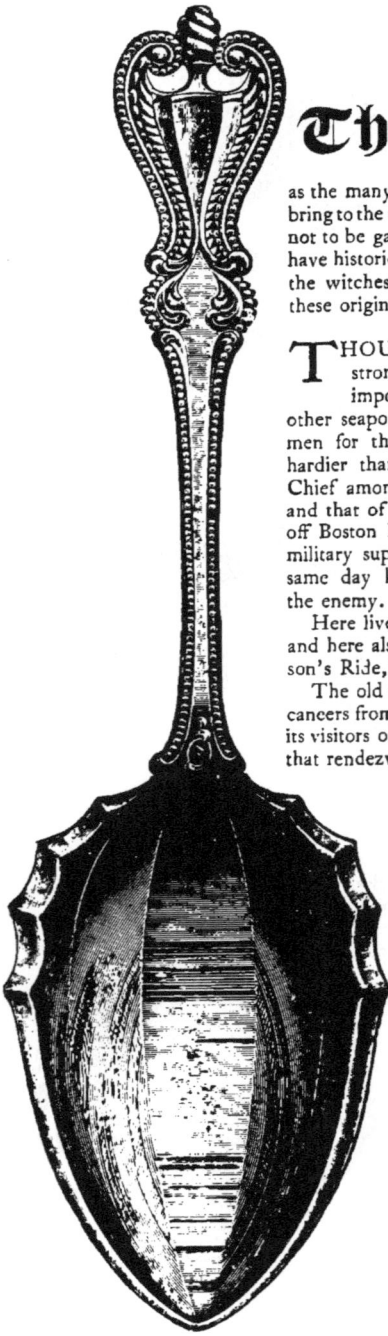

The Colonial Book

as the many other houses and haunts immortalized in his writings, bring to the thoughtful visitor a vivid sense of personal acquaintance, not to be gained alone by the reading of his works. Other cities have historic associations and fine old architecture, have had even the witches — of painful memory — but only Salem can show these originals of storied scenes.

THOUGH small in point of population, Marblehead has strongly marked characteristics, and has played a very important part in the history of our country. Like the other seaport towns of northern Massachusetts, it furnished many men for the navy of the Revolution, and none were braver or hardier than the sons of this rocky and picturesque hamlet. Chief among these was Captain Mugford, to whose memory and that of his crew a memorial has been erected. He captured, off Boston harbor, in May, 1776, a British ship, laden with military supplies; but, after sending this safely to port, was the same day killed, while defending his ship against an attack of the enemy.

Here lived Agnes Surriage, beloved of Sir Henry Frankland, and here also is the scene of Whittier's poem of "Skipper Ireson's Ride," though the story is doubtless largely imaginary.

The old town is said to have been a resort of pirates and buccaneers from the Spanish Main, but it is pleasanter to contemplate its visitors of to-day, the magnificent yachts that rendezvous here from the coast.

Powder House
Marblehead

House where First Sunday School in America was Instituted: 1810. Beverly

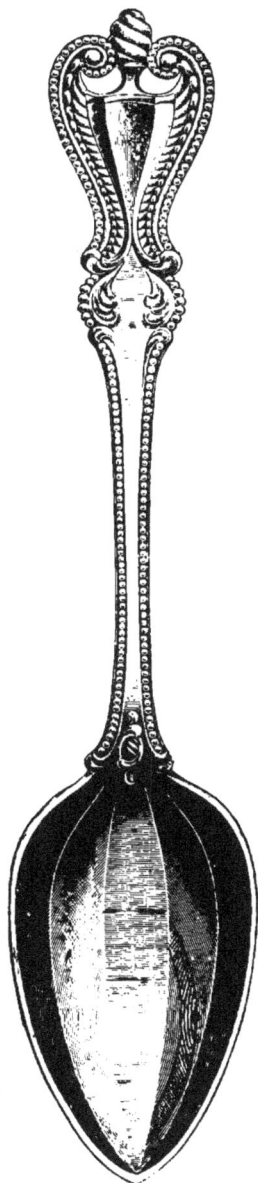

A CROSS the harbor from Marblehead is Beverly, the two
arranged like sentinels, guarding the approach to Salem,
which is further inland. Marblehead and Beverly divide
other honors, for the regiment commanded by Colonel Glover
was recruited from both places, and took an active part in the
Revolution. It was at one time stationed at Beverly, to cover
the movements of British men-of-war lying in the outer harbor.
This regiment was frequently selected by Washington for enterprises requiring great courage and skill, as instanced by its responsible part in the evacuation of New York by the American army
in 1776. Its most notable achievement, however, was the
memorable passage of the Delaware, when, on the night of
Christmas, 1776, Washington's army was enabled, under the
skillful guidance of these men of Marblehead and Beverly, to
cross in safety the stormy and ice-filled river, and capture at
Trenton a large part of the British army.

Beverly was bombarded by the British ship Nautilus, but
suffered no great damage. In return, her privateers, which were
early commissioned, brought in many valuable prizes and materially aided the American cause.

A T the time of the Revolution and for the first half of this
century, the whole of Cape Ann was known as Gloucester. Since that time the towns of Rockport and Annisquam
have been set off, thus reducing the territory of Gloucester.

Fishing, in which it is now supreme, has always been its leading industry, and the "Captains Courageous" of Kipling were no
less so when courage meant the braving of hostile guns as well as
tempest and rocky shores.

The Colonial Book

A Newburyport privateer, the Yankee Hero, reinforced by Gloucester sailors, was captured, off the Cape, by a British man-of-war, disguised as a merchantman, after a hard fought battle. Among the noted patriots of those days, Captain Harraden of Gloucester was a famous and successful fighter who did great service for his country.

On the southerly side of the entrance to Gloucester harbor, lies the reef of Norman's Woe—remembered in Longfellow's "Wreck of the Hesperus"—the ceaseless peal of the floating bell warning the mariner of its menacing presence, as when, on that fatal night of old, the skipper's daughter cried:—

> "O father! I hear the church-bells ring,
> O say, what may it be?"

ONE of the most interesting of neighboring cities is Portsmouth. From the earliest time it has been fortified, and later its fine deep harbor led to the establishment of the Navy Yard and attendant government institutions.

All the prevalent sentiments of liberty and independence noted in accounts of other places were characteristic of Portsmouth, though the town had probably a greater number of prominent loyalists than any other, save Boston. They were roughly handled by the patriots, and at the outbreak of open hostilities were obliged to seek safety elsewhere.

One of the first decisive acts of the Revolution, if not the first, was successfully consummated here, on the night of December 14, 1774, four months before the battle of Lexington.

On that night, a party of men, anticipating the garrisoning of Fort William and Mary, at Newcastle, by the forces of the king, descended on the fort, surprising and overpowering the sentinel and commandant, forced its surrender, and removed to Portsmouth upwards of one hundred barrels of gunpowder and fifteen of the lightest cannon. The munitions were effectively used in the Revolution, a large part of the gunpowder being sent to Cambridge.

Portsmouth was markedly aristocratic in early times, and the elegant Colonial mansions that still adorn its streets are reminders of the days of affluence, when, like Newburyport and Salem, it gloried in a large foreign trade or hoarded the gains of privateering.

The Colonial Book

HAVERHILL, which is to-day a populous and busy city, lacked the advantages of the coast towns, and although settled in 1640, did not reach its present development until the era of manufacturing had superseded that of commerce. It was, however, notably active in the events leading up to the Revolution, and furnished, both promptly and willingly, its full quota of men and funds for that war.

In earlier times, Haverhill suffered severely from Indian attacks, its inland situation rendering it particularly liable to this danger. The most famous of these took place on the fifteenth of March, 1697, when thirty-nine persons were killed or captured, and a number of houses burned.   Among those taken prisoners were, Hannah Duston—whose husband, Thomas Duston, fought his way to safety, with seven of their eight children—and Mary Neff, her nurse.   After traveling some days and suffering many hardships, they were brought to an island in the Merrimac, situated a few miles above what is now Concord.   Early on the morning of April 30, while the savages all slept, Mrs. Duston aroused her nurse and an English youth who had been longer a prisoner, and, arming themselves with tomahawks, they killed their captors, to the number of ten, a squaw and youth escaping. After scuttling all the canoes but one, they provisioned that and started back to Haverhill, but, before going far, decided to return and scalp the Indians, as evidence of their deed; this they did, finally reaching home in safety.   One of the features of Haverhill is the Hannah Duston monument commemorating this event.

A FEW miles from Newburyport, in the town of Amesbury, is the home of Whittier's later years, and from there, in 1892, he was buried, the simple service attended by a gathering of genius such as few occasions could attract.

An interesting reminder of Whittier, in Amesbury, is the "Captain's Well," the subject of his poem of that name.

It was constructed by Captain Bagley, in or about 1794.

> "I will dig a well for the passers-by,
> And none shall suffer from thirst, as I."

A S active revolution had its beginning in the battles of Concord and Lexington, battles which filled the roads from far and near with hurrying minute-men, pressing

The Colonial Book

eagerly to the aid of their heroic compatriots, we have included illustrations of a few of the many historic buildings and commemorative monuments identified with this uprising, with which these towns abound.

All the towns here written of, and many others, share in a degree, with Concord and Lexington, the glory of these monuments; for, while only those favored by proximity arrived in time to take part in the fighting, all responded immediately to the alarm.

SOME PLACES OF HISTORIC INTEREST IN NEWBURYPORT AND VICINITY WHICH MAY BE REACHED BY ELECTRIC CARS. NEWBURYPORT IS SITUATED AT THE MOUTH OF THE MERRIMAC RIVER, WHICH JOINS THE ATLANTIC ON THE NORTH SHORE OF MASSACHUSETTS BAY, THIRTY-SEVEN MILES FROM BOSTON, AND IS REACHED BY TWO DIVISIONS OF THE BOSTON AND MAINE RAILROAD, FROM THE NORTHERN UNION STATION, CAUSEWAY STREET, BOSTON.

Parker river, named for Rev. Thomas Parker, one of the first settlers who landed on its north shore in 1635. About four miles from railroad station.

The Colonial Book

The picturesque Spencer-Pierce house, also called the "Garrison House," built by Daniel Pierce about 1670, on a farm of four hundred acres laid out to John Spencer in 1635.

"Trayneing Green," laid out in 1642. Scene of the encampment of Quebec expedition under Benedict Arnold, September, 1775, and location of a boulder and bronze tablet commemorating the event.

The Noyes house on Parker Street, built about the year 1646 by Rev. James Noyes associate pastor with Rev. Thomas Parker. Near by is the old elm of Newbury, a tree of romantic origin, and the subject of a poem by Hannah Flagg Gould.

The Coffin house, High Street, occupied by Tristram Coffin, in 1653, and afterwards the residence of Joshua Coffin, the historian of Newbury, also remembered as Whittier's "Village Schoolmaster." Still occupied by descendants of the original owner.

The Illsley house, High Street, near head of Marlborough Street, built in 1670, and at one time a tavern. Near by, from 1653 to 1755, was the Blue Anchor Tavern, the most important of early inns.

House No. 65 High Street, owned and occupied by Caleb Cushing at the time of his death.

First Presbyterian meeting house, Federal Street, erected in 1756 and rebuilt in 1856. Here Rev. George Whitefield, the great evangelist, preached and was buried, in a vault under the pulpit.

Nos. 3 and 5 School Street, the house where William Lloyd Garrison was born.

Nos. 9 and 11 School Street, the house where Rev. George Whitefield died.

Bomb-shell, on a stone post at the corner of Middle and Independence Streets. Brought from Louisburg by Nathaniel Knapp, after the capture of that fortress, in 1758.

Market Square. On the southeasterly side stood the house owned by William Morse, whose wife, Goody Morse, was, in 1679, convicted of witchcraft and sentenced to death; but, the people becoming more enlightened, the sentence was not executed.

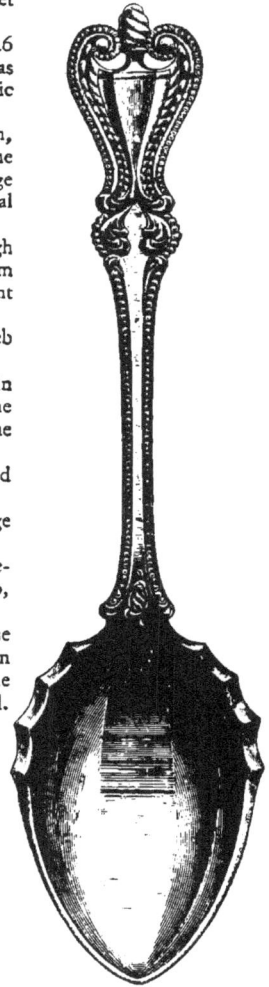

The Colonial Book

This was probably the first case of trial and conviction for witchcraft in Massachusetts.

Rooms of Newburyport Marine Society, State Street, organized in 1772; containing curiosities gathered by members. Open to visitors from 10 to 12 A. M., 2 to 4 P. M.

No. 21 Charter Street, for many years the residence of Hannah Flagg Gould, author of several volumes of prose and poetry.

Public Library building, erected in 1771 by Patrick Tracy, a prominent merchant, as a residence for his son, Nathaniel Tracy, also a merchant and ship owner who attained wide prominence by reason of the magnitude of his operations and the magnificence of his living. Washington occupied apartments in this house in 1789, and Lafayette was entertained here in 1824. In 1865 the building was purchased and adapted for the present use, and was added to in 1882, by the generosity of Michael Simpson. On the first floor are: a free reading room, maintained for many years through the liberality of William C. Todd, Esq., and the rooms of the Historical Society of Old Newbury, where visitors may inspect objects of historic interest. Some of the rooms on this floor retain their original character.

Dalton house, No 95 State Street, built in 1750, and occupied by Tristriam Dalton, the first senator to congress from Massachusetts. Was later occupied by Moses Brown, a wealthy merchant. Now owned and occupied by the Dalton Club.

Frog Pond and Bartlett Mall, now included in Washington Park, were first improved in 1800, through the exertions and liberality of Captain Edmund Bartlett.

The Court House stands on this Mall, and nearly opposite is the Putnam Free School building, one of the earliest and most liberal institutions of its kind. At the easterly end of the Park is a statue of Washington by J. Q. A. Ward, presented to the city by Daniel I. Tenney.

House No. 34 Green Street, built in 1879 by Hon. Theophilus Parsons, an eminent jurist, with whom John Quincy Adams and Robert Treat Paine studied law, and occupied by him until 1800.

Marshes
Plum Island

Brown Square, given to the city by Moses Brown in 1802. The statue of William Lloyd Garrison was presented to the city by William H. Swasey, Esq., and is by David M. French of Newburyport.

Meeting house of the First Religious Society, Pleasant Street, built in 1800. A fine example of early architecture, with characteristic interior.

High Street, St. Paul's Church. The first building was erected here in 1738, and was taken down in the year 1800, to make room for the present edifice. Right Rev. Edward Bass, D.D., was at that time rector of the church, and was the first bishop of the diocese of Massachusetts and Rhode Island. It has many interesting architectural features, and also a bell made by Paul Revere.

Dexter house, No. 201 High Street, built by Jonathan Jackson in 1772, and later purchased and occupied by "Lord" Timothy Dexter, a wealthy and eccentric character, by whom it was adorned with many wooden statues, since removed. It was purchased in 1874 by Mr. George H. Corliss, the renowned engine builder, and occupied by his family until recently.

Lowell-Johnson house, No. 203 High Street, built about 1774 by John Lowell, son of Rev. John Lowell, who was afterwards judge of the United States Circuit Court. He was the father of Francis Cabot Lowell, for whom the city of Lowell was named, grandfather of the founder of the Lowell Institute of Boston, and also grandfather of James Russell Lowell. The house was later occupied by John Tracy, son of Patrick Tracy, and he entertained here, in 1782, the Marquis de Castellux, Baron Talleyrand, and other officers of the French army.

House No. 244 High Street, frequently the home of John G. Whittier during the last years of his life.

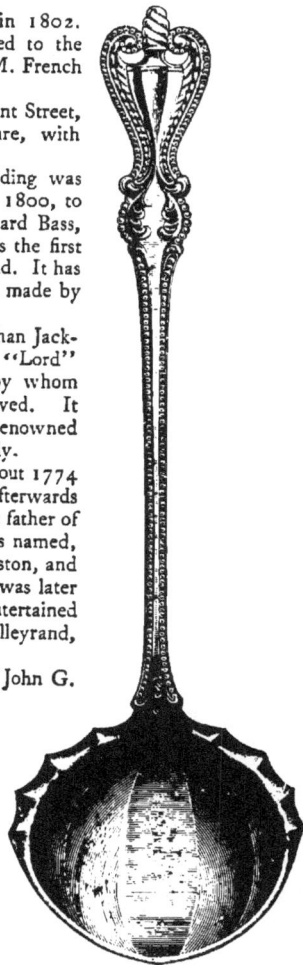

Moulton Castle

Little River Bridge

The Toppan house, No. 10 Toppan Street, built by Jacob Toppan in 1670, and still in possession of his lineal descendants.

House northeasterly corner of Oakland and High Streets, was owned and occupied by James Parton.

Pillsbury place, No. 265 High Street. This was first the farm of Edward Rawson, clerk of the town and member of the House of Deputies. Later, he was for thirty-five years secretary of the Colony of Massachusetts Bay. In 1651 it was by him sold to Job C. Pillsbury, who in 1700 erected a dwelling house, which was destroyed by fire in 1889, and of which the present structure, owned and occupied by his descendants, is a copy.

Essex, Merrimac, or "Chain" Bridge. Here in 1792 was erected the first bridge across the Merrimac river. It was, in 1810, superseded by the present suspension bridge, which was the second of its kind in the country.

Deer Island, home of Harriet Prescott Spofford. The house here was, in the early part of the century, a noted tavern and toll-house for the bridges on either side.

Garrison House
Haverhill

The Colonial Book

Among the most interesting spots to be found are the old burial grounds with their curious and quaintly inscribed head-stones, memorials in many cases of famous characters, and in themselves a written history of many early events. Those most easily reached are: —

The Burying Ground of the First Parish, High Street, near "Trayneing Green." Many of the first settlers are buried here.

The Old Hill Burying Ground and the New Hill Burying Ground, both on Pond Street, near Washington Park. Here are buried many once prominent in local and national affairs.

St. Paul's Church-yard, High Street.

Burying Ground of the Second Parish, Sawyer's Hill.

Belleville Cemetery, formerly churchyard of Queen Anne's Chapel, the first building of the Episcopal Church.

Oak Hill Cemetery, State Street, consecrated in 1842, is the most important modern burying ground, and is noteworthy for the beauty of its situation and arrangement, as well as for its entrance gates and many fine monuments.

For much of the information contained in the above list the compiler is indebted to a volume entitled, "OULD NEWBURY," by John J. Currier. Published by Damrell and Upham, Boston, Mass.

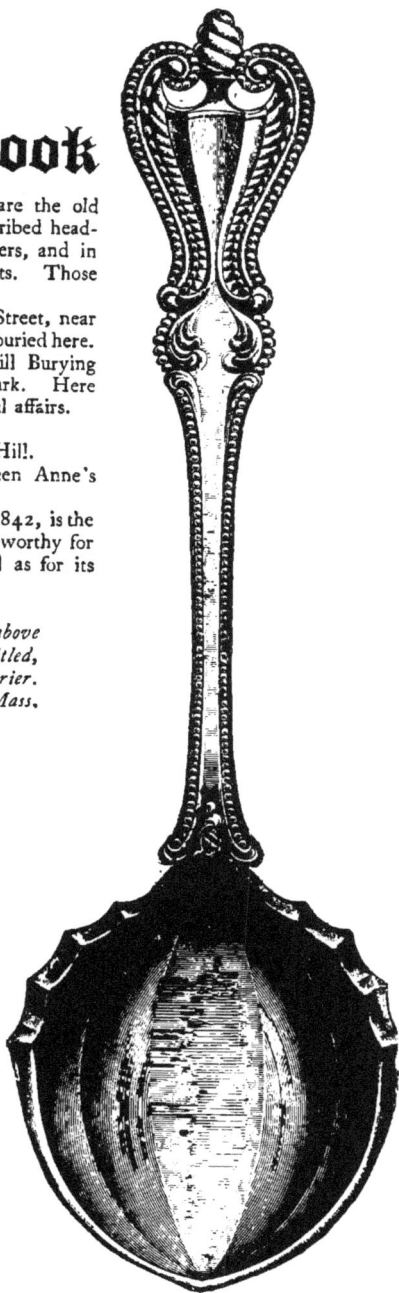

This little book was arranged and printed for the
TOWLE MFG. COMPANY, *Silversmiths*
by WILL BRADLEY, *at the* UNIVERSITY PRESS
Cambridge, U. S. A.

One Hundred and Sixtieth Thousand